ON THE SIGNIFICANCE OF RELIGION IN IMMIGRATION POLICY

The pervasive role religion plays in immigration policy is universally acknowledged but not well understood. *On the Significance of Religion in Immigration Policy* explores the ways in which religion affects immigration policy, focusing on two Abrahamic religions: Christianity and Judaism. This cutting-edge volume:

- Makes sense of the varied roles played by two Abrahamic religions in immigration policy and practice.
- Shows how distinguishing between religion as belief/practice and religion as national identity can serve as a heuristic tool in understanding how religion affects immigration policy.
- Investigates scriptural passages relevant to immigration, their reception history, and how they have been used to justify diverse policies. Uses case studies to provide an overview of the complex and varied religious responses to immigrants.
- Offers policy implications for understanding the religious impact on immigration for policymakers, practitioners, and academics.

Applying cutting-edge research to concrete situations, this volume provides an accessible and concise overview suitable for academics, policymakers, and practitioners alike, building a common platform for understanding how some of the major world religions treat the stranger in both theory and practice.

Barnabas Aspray is Assistant Professor of Systematic Theology at St. Mary's Seminary and University, where he teaches doctrine of god, christology, ecumenism, interfaith relations, and fundamental theology. He is interested in the way Christian belief and practice interact with the concerns and questions of contemporary Western society and is committed to making theology accessible and relevant to everyday life outside academia. He is the founding host of the "Faith at the Frontiers" podcast.

David Elcott was trained in political psychology and Middle East affairs at Columbia University and in Judaic studies at the American Jewish University. Dr. Elcott served as the Taub Professor of Practice in Public Service and Leadership at the Wagner School of Public Service at NYU, directing the advocacy and political action specialization. He is now a Columbia University–SUNY professor teaching incarcerated college degree students at a maximum-security prison as part of a program run by Hudson Link for Higher Education in Prison.

Religion Matters: On the Significance of Religion in Global Issues

Edited by Christine Schliesser
Zurich University, Switzerland
S. Ayse Kadayifci-Orellana
Georgetown University, USA and
Pauline Kollontai
York St. John University, UK.

Policy makers, academics and practitioners worldwide are increasingly paying attention to the role of religion in global issues. This development is clearly noticeable in conflict resolution, development or climate change, to name just a few pressing issues of global relevance. Up to now, no book series has yet attempted to analyze the role of religion in current global issues in a coherent and systematic way that pertains to academics, policy makers and practitioners alike. The Sustainable Development Goals (SDGs) serve as a dynamic frame of reference. "Religion Matters" provides cutting edge scholarship in a concise format and accessible language, thereby addressing academics, practitioners and policy makers.

On the Significance of Religion for the SDGs: An Introduction
Christine Schliesser

On the Significance of Religion for Human Rights
Pauline Kollontai and Friedrich Lohmann

On the Significance of Religion in Climate Change
Kalzang Dorjee Bhutia, Youssef Chouhoud, Lan T. Chu, and Amy Holmes-Tagchungdarpa

On the Significance of Religion in Immigration Policy
Barnabas Aspray and David Elcott

For more information about this series, please visit: www.routledge.com/religion/series/RELMAT

ON THE SIGNIFICANCE OF RELIGION IN IMMIGRATION POLICY

Barnabas Aspray and David Elcott

LONDON AND NEW YORK

Designed cover image: 'Fragmente' by Schwarzfalter GmbH
www.schwarzfalter.ch

First published 2026
by Routledge
4 Park Square, Milton Park, Abingdon, Oxon OX14 4RN

and by Routledge
605 Third Avenue, New York, NY 10158

Routledge is an imprint of the Taylor & Francis Group, an informa business

© 2026 Barnabas Aspray and David Elcott

The right of Barnabas Aspray and David Elcott to be identified as authors of this work has been asserted in accordance with sections 77 and 78 of the Copyright, Designs and Patents Act 1988.

All rights reserved. No part of this book may be reprinted or reproduced or utilised in any form or by any electronic, mechanical, or other means, now known or hereafter invented, including photocopying and recording, or in any information storage or retrieval system, without permission in writing from the publishers.

Trademark notice: Product or corporate names may be trademarks or registered trademarks, and are used only for identification and explanation without intent to infringe.

British Library Cataloguing-in-Publication Data
A catalogue record for this book is available from the British Library

ISBN: 978-1-032-64517-9 (hbk)
ISBN: 978-1-032-64519-3 (pbk)
ISBN: 978-1-032-64520-9 (ebk)

DOI: 10.4324/9781032645209

Typeset in Sabon
by Apex CoVantage, LLC

CONTENTS

Acknowledgments   *ix*
Executive Summary and Recommendations   *xi*

   Introduction   1

   Why Immigration Matters 1
   Why Religion Matters 2
   Scope of This Book 7
   Methodology 8
   Outline of This Book 9

1 Judaism and Immigration Policy   14

   Jewish Law, Jewish Values, and Jewish
     Attitudes: Contradictions Abound 15
   Israel Addresses Who Is Authentic 21
   Jews in the Diaspora 24
   Immigration, Jewish Purity, and Jewish
     Caring for the Stranger 26

2 Christianity and Immigration Policy   31

   Basic Christian Principles 32
   Christians in Europe: Past and Present 35
   Catholic Immigration Policy Today 49

A Brief Note on the Orthodox Church 53
American Evangelicals and the Bible 54
Immigration in the Bible 57
Conclusion 67

3 A Jewish Case Study   77

The State of Israel Is Unique 78
Among the Nations: The Jewish Minority in the United States 84
Conclusion 88

4 A Christian Case Study: The 2015 Refugee "Crisis"   91

Introduction 91
A Brief Sketch of Events 91
Answering the Question "Why?" 93
Viktor Orbán and Hungary 95
Angela Merkel and Germany 101
Conclusion 105

Now What? Implications for Academics, Policymakers, and Practitioners   110

A Vignette: Pope Francis, J.D. Vance, and the Ordo Amoris *111*
Final Recommendations 113

Index   118

ACKNOWLEDGMENTS

Barnabas Aspray would like to thank all the people whose passionate commitment to the disadvantaged in society in the name of Jesus has been a source of inspiration, particularly David Hollow, Catherine Gladwell, Joy Johnston, Rachel Davies-Teka, and Nathaniel Aspray. I would also like to thank my dear friends who are less inclined to see Christianity as supporting immigrant welcome. Their constant challenge to my views has pushed me to clarify and deepen my analysis, and I hope they feel that their position is equally, fairly, and fully represented in this book.

David Elcott is the child of asylum-seeking refugees, so interest in immigration comes to me honestly. My mother fled Germany, where Nazi anti-Semitism threatened her and eventually murdered much of our family. My father's family wandered to escape persecution and economic collapse until they found a home in the tenements of Harlem. They all worked in sweatshops and factories with faith in American democracy and opportunity. I may have been born into poverty, yet, as a family, we managed to flourish. My children and grandchildren were born into an America enriched by its immigrants, a land in which religious freedom has been the norm for centuries. We are now engaged in a time of conflict over the core values of America, magnified in nations around the world, as they all struggle to clarify who is a real citizen, who belongs, and who should be excluded. So coauthoring this book is also an affirmation of hope that the grandchildren I love – and children and grandchildren across the globe – will find safe havens that respect and appreciate an inclusive religious and ethnic diversity that enriches us all.

Many thanks from both authors to Pembroke College, Oxford, and the "Religion and the Frontier Challenges" research program, where much of the research for this volume was done. It is also where the authors first met and had a vigorous discussion about immigration. Thanks to Fr. Maximilian Jaskowak, O.P., and Matthew Dugandzic for reading drafts of the chapters on Christianity and providing feedback. Special thanks go to Alex Faludy, who kindly read a draft of the Christian "case study" chapter and whose expertise on the religious situation in Hungary proved invaluable.

We would also like to thank the series editors, Christine Schliesser, Pauline Kollontai, and Ayse Kadayifci-Orellana, for their helpful feedback, which has served to improve and refine the volume.

Finally, the authors would like to thank Sadia Kidwai and Zeyneb Sayilgan for their dialog throughout the writing of this book and for offering an Islamic take on immigration. Even though circumstances conspired to prevent them from contributing to their final form, their insights and reflections have been helpful in enlarging our understanding of immigration from a broader Abrahamic perspective.

EXECUTIVE SUMMARY AND RECOMMENDATIONS

The most important insight from this book concerns the relationship between religious identity and national identity and the significant impact this relationship has on immigration policies around the world. A religious community has the right to exclude those who do not subscribe to the religion's beliefs and practices, nor does anybody expect them to do otherwise. But a religious community does not necessarily have national territory and borders. When it is increasingly identified with a particular territory, its exclusivity can take on sinister forms, leading to hostile immigration policies. Yet, while both religions represented in this book can have exclusionary reflexes, they also contain multiple injunctions to welcome the stranger, and those who spend time in the scriptural and traditional sources cannot avoid this message. The question becomes how these faiths and the faithful relate to and influence national immigration policy.

The following implications break down and specify this complex issue further.

Implication 1: Understand the Double-Edged Power of Religion

Religion can be a higher allegiance than any political, racial, cultural, or ethnic community. This is a double-edged fact. On the one hand, it means that religious sources have priority over the interests of the nation-state in seeking moral guidance on immigration policy. On the other hand, this allegiance can lead to a loyalty to fellow believers that excludes and ostracizes the religious "other." Both these effects of religious devotion can be seen in history and in the present day.

Implication 2: Distinguish Two Conceptions of Religiosity

Religious people can understand their religiosity in two (not mutually exclusive) ways that are relevant for immigration: as communal/national identity and as a set of beliefs and practices. A broad trend, not without exceptions, shows that hostility toward immigrants arises more frequently from those who construe their religion in terms of communal/national identity, whereas welcome of immigrants arises more frequently among those who spend more time in religious practice, which includes reflecting on the scriptural and traditional sources of moral guidance. Israel is an exception, where there is more scriptural warrant for policies that are hostile to immigration.

Implication 3: Notice the Overlap Between Religion and Nationality

Hostility to immigrants is strongest among citizens who see an overlap between their religion and their nationality, such that to be a true member of a particular nation-state entails belonging to the nation's majority religion. This was seen starkly in the late Middle Ages and early modern period with the practice of expelling Jews (and in some cases, Muslims) from various European nations in order to establish a complete identity between nationality and faith adherence. In the contemporary period, those who seek such an overlap tend to appeal to the preservation of their culture's traditional values, which are often rooted in their religious heritage but not always in religious belief or practice.

Implication 4: Encourage the Religious to Engage With Their Scriptures

For both Christianity and Judaism, holy text is at the core of faith as the word of God. And scripture is, therefore, often used to justify a particular immigration policy, whether in support of or to denounce immigration and immigrants. It is an important reminder to those who make or endorse policy that while one set of religious texts can be a pretext for justifying policy in most cases, there will be other texts to support an opposite policy position. Yet a trend has emerged, not without exceptions, that those with a deeper familiarity and more sustained engagement with their religion's scriptures are more likely to adopt a welcoming stance toward vulnerable immigrants.

INTRODUCTION

Why Immigration Matters

More people than ever before are on the move, making immigration arguably the most hotly contested issue facing policymakers and voters around the world. From India to the United States and Israel to France, immigration is at the forefront of topics in election campaigns. But migration has been a reality since the dawn of human history, and displacement due to war or famine is nothing new. What makes migration so prevalent today? We suggest four main reasons for the current surge in migration:

1. The rising global population has brought with it record levels of migration, including forced migration. By the end of 2024, there were over 120 million forcibly displaced people in the world, according to the United Nations High Commissioner for Refugees (UNHCR). This is to say nothing of the levels of unforced migration.
2. The effects of global warming are making parts of the world uninhabitable, compelling whole societies to flee and seek a home elsewhere. Every prediction reminds us that the number of "climate refugees" will grow in the coming decades (Chazalnoël & Randall 2022).
3. The modern nation-state system has left no corner of the habitable world unclaimed or unprotected. When people leave one

nation, they have no option but to enter another, legally or otherwise (Aleinikoff & Zamore 2019: 1).
4. Wealth disparity between nations compels many in poorer parts of the world with scarce job opportunities to migrate for the purpose of securing better or more stable economic prospects.

Why Religion Matters

This volume contends that it is impossible to understand the immigration policies of most nations without deepening our awareness of the role of religion.

The word "religion" may conjure up images of steeples and minarets, holy places with the faithful in prayer. To others, it suggests beliefs about the afterlife or God. Both these obscure important insights about religion, which has never been limited to personal piety. As Kwame Appiah says, "religion is not, in the first instance, a matter of belief" (Appiah 2018: 23). Religion is about belonging and affects one's identity, one's place in the world, and one's sense of home. It is often linked to national identity, either formally, where the nation enshrines a specific religion, or informally as the faith of the majority. This is where it can influence immigration policy powerfully, since, as McDaniel et al. write, "cultural issues [of which religion is a large component] have a more robust effect on immigration attitudes than economic issues" (McDaniel et al. 2011: 209).

On a deeper level, religion can be a talisman for meaningful levels of cultural integration, establishing a sense of authenticity and belonging or hostile ostracization of those who do not share the majority's religious tradition. Likewise, religious teaching about social justice, compassion, and the welcome of strangers can be a powerful motivating force for people to show solidarity with immigrants in numerous ways. In short, religion is a powerful influence on public *attitudes* toward foreigners, providing reasons both to justify exclusion and to provide welcome. Religion thus forms a motivating factor determining party platforms, mobilizing popular sentiment, and affecting voting patterns, all of which give rise to policy.

In the introduction to this series, Schliesser (2023: xv) outlines seven dimensions of religion. In this book, we focus on two of these that have the most relevance for immigration policy:

1. Religion as an element in forming national, communal, and/or cultural identity.
2. Religion as a set of intertwined beliefs and practices that include a range of ethical commitments.

This does not imply that all common identities are religious, still fewer beliefs and moral codes. But all religions, as typically understood, have both elements. We will not attempt to give a precise and all-encompassing definition of religion since such an enterprise is fraught with difficulties (see Cavanaugh 2009). Instead, these two of the many ways people understand their own religiosity can serve as a heuristic tool to guide us in making sense of the practical ways the word is used in debates on immigration policy. Similarly, we do not think it is worth separating "belief" from "practice" to make three dimensions of religion. This is because if belief is completely separated from practice, then it becomes irrelevant to immigration policy. The only time immigration policy is affected by a religious belief is if that belief is also practiced. Conversely, a practice always contains an implied belief concerning it, even if that belief has not been articulated.

Religions often make an exclusive claim on their adherents. While in antiquity (e.g., in the Roman Empire) a person could belong to multiple religions in the same way as one might join several social clubs, others offer more than wise advice or social customs. They demand ultimate allegiance to the religious community, to specific defined behaviors, and to the ethical commitments contained in their teachings.

Religion is powerful, but it is also open to misuse. Indeed, to "use" religion for another (political) purpose is to distort its meaning. To call something "useful" means that it serves some other end. But religion claims for itself the end and purpose of all other activities. Religion (as belief/practice) offers answers to the "why" behind all ethical action: why are certain actions good or bad, right or wrong, commendable or detestable? Why should anyone look beyond their material interests to the interests of others? Why should concern for the well-being of others interfere with an individual's pleasures, wealth, and wants? And (crucially for the purpose of immigration policy) why should an individual go beyond their instinctual concern for their family and neighbors to show concern for the "other," the outsider, the stranger? However, the nonreligious may or may not answer these questions; for the religious, the answers are found in their religion's teachings.

Religion's capacity to answer life's ultimate questions explains why, in predominantly religious parts of the world, politics cannot be separated from religion. From Nigeria to Indonesia, Myanmar to India, and Israel to Poland, religion dominates the debates over a wide range of policy decisions. Those who call for a separation of religion and politics do so because they often have been burned by the experience of an unhealthy relationship between the two: namely, when religion is made into something "useful" to serve political ends.

Yet to say that religion often demands ultimate allegiance does not mean that every self-identifying member recognizes these demands. The category of "nonpracticing" or "nominal" is well-known. Atheists and agnostics can still identify with a religious heritage that seems natural to those living in that community, enjoying public holiday celebrations and customs outside any formal religious setting. Still, what may come as a surprise to some is that religion also remains a driving force in highly secularized societies. This is because, even when people no longer self-identify as religious, they often retain elements of their religious heritage, both as communal identity and as ethical commitments.

Let us first consider the ways religion as communal identity continues to influence the secular world. In *Is God Back?*, Hjelm (2015) challenges traditional notions of the role religion plays in the public square. Considering people whose religious fervor is inextricably linked to their patriotic nationalist fervor, he suggests:

> The blunt answer is "no." To put it differently: religion, not God, is back. There is an internal secularization of discourse, if you will, at work in the new visibility of religion. . . . It is

their public activity which is its focus, not the interior life of faith itself, nor the religious reasons or goals which motivate it. Religion is visible . . . , but God has little to do with it.

(Hjelm 2015: 15)

The religion Hjelm describes is about wedding patriotic symbols to the historic religious identity of a nation (think of so many national flags with crosses, with the Muslim crescent, or with the Jewish Star of David), symbols that connect citizens to their cherished past, a world in which the divine is manifest in the religious iconography of the nation. And even if the divine is no longer obviously present, the symbols can remain potent.

But the second meaning of religion – ethical commitments and practices – can also remain in a secularized society. Many people hold on to a moral position long after losing sight of the original religious reasons for it. Much of the distinctive ethical stance of Europe and North America has its roots in Christian morality, and this continues to be the case even in nations with low church attendance.

It is the ultimacy of allegiance that gives rise to the ambiguous and conflicting effect of religion on immigration policy. When we speak as we did above of the structures of religion that create a sense of identity and loyalty to the community, maintaining those deep connections to those with whom that loyalty and identity are shared, that loyalty can take an exclusive attitude against nonmembers. But when we consider the voice of religion, life's meaning offered in scripture, sermons, and rituals, all the world's major religions contain injunctions about how to positively treat nonmembers, often involving welcome, support, and inclusivity.

There is a paradox here, a serious tension, that goes to the heart of communal identity and shows the interconnectedness of all these dimensions of religion. The very notion of "common identity" implies characteristics that a group holds in common – whether ethnicity, beliefs, practices, or anything else. No community can be radically inclusive of those who do not share those characteristics without threatening its coherence. Even if it holds "inclusivity" as its highest value, the community may still exclude those who would rupture the bonds of loyalty to the community. Debates rage in France over whether wearing religious garb undermines the laïcité at the core of French identity or whether allowing Arabic to have equal standing with Hebrew challenges the Jewish identity of Israel. For many, Hindutva, a movement that demands the exclusivity of Hindu domination in India or the expulsion of Muslims from Buddhist Myanmar, is crucial to sustaining national identity. In short, no community of any kind, religious or otherwise, can be radically inclusive and retain a meaningful identity. It draws boundaries. Those who do not share the features that make up the unique communal identity are "other." What the community then needs to determine is how it will treat those nonmembers.

It should be clear that our focal dimensions of religion, its structures and its meaning and purpose, cannot help but have implications for immigration policy. To restate, religion as a common identity shapes attitudes of inclusivity/exclusivity toward outsiders. Many nations of the world have traditionally been associated with one or more of the world's major religions, and many of their inhabitants continue to identify with a religion even if their beliefs and practices do not conform to it. The communal and institutional dimension of religion, even if the religion is not formally the nation's faith, cannot be fully dissociated from national and international politics. A nation's traditional religious affiliation is part of the web of a shared, treasured culture. Anyone immigrating from outside can easily be seen as a threat to that sense of "at-homeness," leading to varying levels of hostility and reluctance to welcome strangers, in our case, refugees, asylum seekers, and migrants seeking a better life.

Similarly, religion as ethical commitment can call adherents to love and welcome the stranger, determining the attitude of the religious individual toward outsiders, whether welcoming or otherwise. That is why the teachings of any religion, especially those found in its sacred texts, can have such a powerful influence not only on how the religious individual votes or what policies they believe to be best but also over those whose national identity is wrapped up in a national culture that includes the religious past of the nation. Here, we pointedly see the tensions between identity and welcome with which political leaders, policymakers, and voters struggle. Leuștean explains how religion is

> instrumentalized by state authorities for specific political goals, while, concomitantly, religious actors provide identity, support and comfort for displaced populations. The ambivalent force of religion is evident in endorsing violence, whether physical or symbolic, as well as finding the means of resilience, reconciliation and conflict resolution.
>
> *(Leuștean 2019: 8)*

Scope of This Book

Today's politics tends to divide people into two camps: those who are "pro-immigration" and those who are "anti-immigration." While this can be a useful heuristic to capture overall attitudes, it is a caricature of any concrete position. Few people are purely for or against all kinds of immigration. It is fair to say that even the most "pro-immigration" policy will want to restrict entry to an invading foreign army, known terrorists, or even overwhelming numbers. It must make a coherent argument to explain why having foreigners is a valuable benefit to the community. Likewise, even the most "anti-immigration" will welcome those who have sufficient wealth or marketable skills and who are sufficiently similar in ethnicity, culture, language, and values. The real question is what *kind* of immigrants a person or a nation will accept and on what grounds.

The focus of this book is on national immigration policy, not the experiences of immigrants, the causes of migration, or even religious types of migration such as pilgrimages.

First of all, immigration policy is about the conditions for entry into a nation-state. Who is allowed in, who is excluded, and for what reasons?

Second, it concerns the legal status of immigrants who are inside and what is available to them in their new country. Do they have all the same rights as citizens? Can they vote, buy property, and run for office?

Third, apart from the law, citizens may be hospitable or xenophobic toward immigrants. This does not strictly count as "policy," but we will occasionally refer to it because a lot of religious activity toward immigrants, both welcoming and hostile, takes place at the level we might call "political." (We understand "political" to be a broad term that includes all kinds of activities that have an effect on the *polis* and on how people, both citizen and stranger, experience it, even if such activities do not lead to a concrete change to "policy" in the narrower sense.)

Methodology

Three caveats are in order regarding how we ascribe religion to national policy. First, not everything religious people do is religiously motivated. Religious people sleep, eat, and wear clothes not because they are religious but because they are human. Not all the attitudes toward immigrants shown by religious people are a result of their religion. Matthew Rowley makes a similar point about religious violence: "Humans can fight over anything, and they will grasp at whatever resources might aid the struggle. Religion, unsurprisingly, is readily at hand" (Rowley 2024: 27). It is not always clear whether religion itself is the cause of an action or simply an instrument to justify it. Likewise, xenophobia and hospitality are both common features of the human condition found everywhere in the world, regardless of religious persuasion. We do not pretend in this volume that all action by religious people is a result of their religious identity and beliefs. But we do claim that religious motivations are often overlooked in analyses of the reasons for immigration policy.

Second, when ascribing political activity to religious motivations, we do not claim that religion is the *only* cause. There are multiple overlapping motivations for a human action, any one of which can be dressed up as "the" cause that drove the narrative forward. Whenever anyone answers the question "why?" about a historical occurrence, they transform history from a collection of disconnected facts into a *narrative* that is both interesting and hard to prove. A historical narrative is interesting because it yields insight that allows us to take lessons from history that inform decision-making today. It is hard to prove because there is always more than one way to tell the story. The historian is forced to be selective, omitting details for the sake of brevity and coherence. For example, Russia's invasion of Ukraine in 2022 has been plausibly explained as strategic and motivated by economics; it has also been explained as an outworking of Putin's religious convictions about reuniting the Holy Land of Rus (O'Beara 2022; Vovk 2022). Both accounts make sense of Putin's actions, yet neither can be proven. They are not even mutually exclusive.

Third, and relatedly, religion is not always explicit. This volume is not simply a list of occasions when religion has been invoked in politics. Religious motivations can be there though unacknowledged, and they can also be absent though claimed. Politicians rarely give the real reason for their decisions, and it can be expedient to hide or to display religious influence depending on the context. While we take a cue from explicitly religious language in politics, we also undertake deeper analyses of the religious motivations that are sometimes hidden and often overlooked.

Outline of This Book

Like other books in this series, we will use case studies to spotlight the effect of religion on immigration policy. Human beings are religious, with thousands of variations and billions who identify with a specific faith. Religious communities will frequently express strong views about who belongs in their country. From Buddhists expelling Rohingya Muslims in Myanmar and Hindutva doctrine that promotes suppressing Islam in India, to Indonesia's incarceration of Jakarta's Christian mayor for blasphemy and Saudi law that only allows Muslims to become citizens, we know that religion can fuel harsh policies of exclusion and expulsion. For this study, we will focus on Christian and Jewish theologies and their impact in four case studies: Christianity in Hungary and Germany, and Judaism in Israel and the United States.

We will begin with an outline of the teachings of the two religious traditions represented in this volume. Both faiths have a great deal to say about the treatment of the stranger and rely on similar originating narratives, mainly those found in the Bible.

In chronological order of origin, the first two chapters explore the ways that Judaism and Christianity approach immigration from conflict and even eradication of those deemed dangerous to welcoming the stranger as a divine command. Both share the tension of uniting the faithful in a community through exclusion and inclusion. That is why selective approaches to phrases and commands from the sacred texts offer radically different approaches to immigration issues. Neither of the faiths offers a unanimously agreed and unified response to the "other." Policymakers, scholars, and pundits who seek to explain the rhetoric around immigration policy choices will find this section to be a crucial background.

Chapter 1 surveys Jewish theology vis-à-vis immigration, which, while beginning with the Torah, takes us through millennial debates on how a Jewish society should address foreigners seeking residence in an imaginary Jewish kingdom. Theology is a lived experience, so historical events matter, and the discussions of rabbis and scholars over hundreds of years must consider the world in which their people live. We will see how a wounded minority, after over 2,000 years living in the orbit of Christianity and Islam, imagines immigration policies in both a Jewish nation and life in the American diaspora.

The relationship between belief and practice in Christianity is different, holding its adherents to a high standard that is not compromised even when few succeed in living up to it. Chapter 2 surveys popular Christian attitudes and behaviors toward immigrants in Europe and the United States before focusing on two dominant trends: Catholicism's shift from hostility toward the religious "other" in the Middle Ages to a Vatican mandate for immigrant welcome and support, and American Evangelicalism's internal disputes over the biblical message, with dramatic consequences for US politics.

The following two chapters bring us to specific responses to immigration, focusing on the present with Israel as the Jewish state and Hungary and Germany as examples of traditionally Christian nations. In the case of Judaism, an additional focus on American Jews offers an alternative voice of political engagement. These case studies, while far from inclusive of how both faiths address immigration, do highlight the tensions and conflicts within each tradition, allowing us an in-depth exploration of the contemporary world so influenced by robust religious traditions that inform, overtly or subtly, immigration policies.

The epilogue is a reminder that the issue of migration and immigration remains one of the most volatile and contentious areas of debate and conflict in the world. And we assume that the tensions over immigration will only increase as governments rise and fall over the issue. What we hope is that the theologies and case studies presented in this slender volume will help those engaged in the immigration debate, from politicians and policymakers to academic researchers and engaged citizens, to better understand the ways that faith and religious traditions impact the debate and the policies that ensue.

As we survey the world of political actors, of nations, and of faith leaders, policymakers and politicians, influencers, and regular voters, the anger, confusion, compassion, and frustration are evident. There are so many religious voices or those invoking religion that seek to influence immigration policy. Pope Francis calls on Catholics when he writes in his 2024 message for the 110th World Day of Migrants and Refugees that *God*

> identifies himself with men and women on their journey through history, particularly with the least, the poor and the marginalized. . . . For this reason, the encounter with the migrant, as with every brother and sister in need, is also an encounter with Christ.
>
> *(Glatz 2024)*

At the same time, the very Catholic Italian Prime Minister Meloni announced her plan to build new detention centers to hold migrants for up to 18 months; Angela Merkel could preach, "We have learned that tolerance is the soul of Europe" (Carrel 2017), while Markus Söder, the leader of the Bavarian wing of Merkel's own sister political party, ordered that all public buildings hang a cross up prominently "as an expression of Bavaria's historical and cultural character" (Anon 2018).

With so many eyes on the United States, a 2024 Gallup poll claimed that Americans see immigration as the most important issue to address. Newly elected Donald Trump and many of his deeply Christian followers claimed that God saved his life and brought him to power. He also is committed to deporting 25 million foreigners, while the United States Conference of Catholic Bishops and the mainline Protestant churches call on Americans to welcome the immigrant. Meanwhile, immigration was a top issue in bolstering the anti-immigrant right wing in the European Union elections of June (Brenan 2024; Ryder 2024).

For leaders and followers, for those attending religious services, and for those who never set foot in a religious setting, it remains the case that the complex political and societal attitudes toward immigrants are often expressed in terms of religious identity as well as religious values. That is what motivates our writing.

References

Aleinikoff, T. Alexander, and Leah Zamore. (2019). *The Arc of Protection: Reforming the International Refugee Regime.* Stanford: Stanford University Press.

Anon. (2018). "Germany's Bavaria Orders Christian Crosses in All State Buildings". April 25. Viewed from: www.bbc.com/news/world-europe-43892329 [Date accessed: 22 October 2024].

Appiah, Kwame Anthony. (2018). *The Lies That Bind: Rethinking Identity.* London: Profile.

Brenan, Megan. (2024). "Immigration Named Top U.S. Problem for Third Straight Month". *Gallup.Com.* Viewed from: https://news.gallup.com/poll/644570/immigration-named-top-problem-third-straight-month.aspx [Date accessed: 4 November 2024].

Carrel, Paul. (2017). "Merkel Preaches Tolerance, Religious Freedom at Reformation Ceremony". *Reuters*, October 31. Viewed from: www.reuters.com/article/world/merkel-preaches-tolerance religious-freedom-at-reformation-ceremony-idUSKBN1D02Q B/ [Date accessed: 22 October 2024].

Cavanaugh, William T. (2009). *The Myth of Religious Violence: Secular Ideology and the Roots of Modern Conflict.* Oxford: Oxford University Press.

Chazalnoël, Mariam Traore, and Alex Randall. (2022). "Migration and the Slow-Onset Impacts of Climate Change: Taking Stock and Taking Action". *World Migration Report* 2022(1).

Glatz, Carol. (2024). "Encountering a Migrant Is Encountering Christ, Pope Says in Message". *USCCB News*. Viewed from: www.usccb.org/news/2024/encountering-migrant-encountering-christ-pope-says-message [Date accessed: 4 November 2024].

Hjelm, Titus. (2015). *Is God Back?: Reconsidering the New Visibility of Religion*. Bloomsbury Publishing.

Leuștean, Lucian. (2019). *Forced Migration and Human Security in the Eastern Orthodox World*. 1st ed. Routledge.

McDaniel, Eric Leon, Irfan Nooruddin, and Allyson Faith Shortle. (2011). "Divine Boundaries: How Religion Shapes Citizens' Attitudes toward Immigrants". *American Politics Research* 39(1):205–33.

O'Beara, Fearghas. (2022). "Russia's War on Ukraine: The Religious Dimension". *European Parliamentary Research Service*. Viewed from: www.europarl.europa.eu/RegData/etudes/ATAG/2022/729355/EPRS_ATA(2022)729355_EN.pdf [Date accessed: 26 March 2025].

Rowley, Matthew. (2024). *God, Religious Extremism and Violence*. Cambridge: Cambridge University Press.

Ryder, Bridget. (2024). "The Anti-Immigrant Tide Is Rising Ahead of EU Elections, Pushing Voters to the Right". *America Magazine*, June 5. Viewed from: www.americamagazine.org/politics-society/2024/06/05/european-union-pact-migration-asylum-refugees-parliamentary-elections [Date accessed: 4 November 2024].

Schliesser, Christine. (2023). *On the Significance of Religion for the SDGs: An Introduction*. Routledge.

Vovk, Dmytro. (2022). "Religion and the Russian-Ukrainian Conflict". *Talk About: Law and Religion*. Viewed from: https://talkabout.iclrs.org/2022/02/25/religion-and-the-russian--conflict/ [Date accessed: 26 March 2025].

1
JUDAISM AND IMMIGRATION POLICY

> The stranger who resides with you shall be to you as one of your citizens; you shall love him as yourself, for you were strangers in the land of Egypt: I the Lord am your God.
> (Leviticus 19:34 – all biblical citations are either my own translation or from the Jewish Publication Society, 1992)

> However, in the cities of the nations the Lord your God is giving you as an inheritance, do not leave alive anything that breathes. Completely destroy them – the Hittites, Amorites, Canaanites, Perizzites, Hivites and Jebusites – as the Lord your God has commanded you.
> (Deuteronomy 20:17)

Judaism, as one heir of biblical Israel, traces its roots back at least 3,000 years. Its millennia of commentaries and lived experience mean that there is no singular voice, no one interpretation, of the shared commands, values, and behaviors that anchor Jewish tradition (Elcott 1995: 135). The Jewish understanding of religion as a spiritual quest, a way of being, believing, belonging, and doing, is evident in the rich traditions that contemporary Jews have at their disposal when navigating policy issues. Although immigration in the contemporary sense of citizenship laws and borders is not found in the tradition, there is much that Jewish leaders use to justify immigration policies.

The two opening biblical citations of this chapter are excellent examples of the wide latitude in how biblical Israel was expected to treat those who were not Israelite – from welcoming the stranger as a fellow resident to evicting even those who quietly occupied the land destined for Israelite conquest. These two streams of thought, of law and narratives, will flow through Israelite and then Jewish traditions almost as competitors, caring for the stranger and wanting the stranger out of the life of Israel.

This chapter will allow us to experience two radically different views battling each other, neither dominating. This tension will take us from the first moments of Israelite culture and then Jewish identity to the present day in Israel and the United States. Relying on the Bible and on Rabbinic debates that continue to this day, we will explore how Jewish law and narrative create two parallel traditions concerning immigrants seeking to reside in a Jewish country or how they should be welcomed wherever they flee. Since there is a Jewish state where rabbis have significant authority, we turn first to how Judaism has given shape to immigration policy in present-day Israel. This national policy will then be compared to the attitudes of Jews in the diaspora. Finally, we will address the impact of the experience of Jews as a minority on Jewish theology with attention to the Holocaust as a motivating factor to support immigration reform, especially among Jews in the United States.

The Bible repeats 36 times that we must care for the stranger because we understand what it is like to be a wanderer, a refugee. The Exodus remains the founding narrative of the Jewish story, called upon to see themselves in every generation as refugees who fled Egypt. The Bible seems forced to repeat this command because it understands how hard it is to care for one who is obviously "other." It demands empathy from those who themselves underwent "othering" as an oppressed minority in Egypt (Farbiaz n.d.).

One can discern a set of values implied in the biblical commandments. They demand certain types of behavior, yet there are also countervailing values that complicate how a contemporary Jew, a policymaker, influencer, or politician, would try to determine a Jewish response to complex policy issues.

Jewish Law, Jewish Values, and Jewish Attitudes: Contradictions Abound

A commandment calling for removing non-Israelites from the Land of Israel and a commandment to care for those most vulnerable, including the foreigner and the stranger, are both the inheritance of the Jewish people. Moving from biblical texts over 2,500 years old to contemporary Judaism and Israel could seem far-fetched, a stretch of the imagination that these texts could seriously influence contemporary policies and political values. Yet Jews in Israel and in its diaspora use texts and traditions to explain and justify the positions they take on contemporary issues. If we imagine religion as a source of communal identity that provides rituals, behaviors, and values – even a sense of the spiritual, the transcendent – to ground the adherent and fortify a unique Jewish identity, then the past can remain alive as a source of direction in one's life. Being Jewish is more than a religious choice; its theology is never separated from sociology and history. It includes both an ethnic component – this is my people even if I do not follow its precepts – and a historical component, in which Jewish identity has also been determined by its engagement with others, often because of oppression. These commandments and implied values remain in the communal consciousness as sources of debate and inspiration.

The Jewish Bible consists of more than laws and normative behaviors by which to live one's life. Biblical narratives, stories from which Jews derive meaning, sit alongside Torah's commands. The primal origin narrative for Jews is the story of Abraham and Sarah, the ancestral progenitors of the Jewish people. It is a story of migration, of abandoning one's home for a better life. God says to Abraham, "You must migrate from your ancestral home, from your birthplace, from your parents' home, to the land I will show you. And there I will make of you a great nation" (Genesis 12:1–2). There is purpose for this migration, the hope of something better not only for Abraham and Sarah but also for their descendants, for all the generations that will follow. Yet there is also conflict and loss that come with the difficulties of settling in a foreign land. It is remarkable that at the very core of the Jewish narrative is leaving one's whole life behind to ensure a better future for one's family. This story is at the core of Jewish identity, as wandering and the search for home explain much of the story of the Jewish people. This narrative, along with the Exodus, can offer a sense of empathy for the wanderer.

Given the memories of Abraham and Sarah, of the Exodus, later exile, wandering, and expulsions, how can we understand the divine call for genocide, which also appears in these stories, or in any way imagine its application today? As we learn from evolutionary biology, kinship and shared culture are the natural ways communities establish an identity, who belongs and who does not (Haidt 2012: ch. 9). This insight perhaps helps us understand what underpins the biblical command to utterly wipe out all those foreign elements who would live within the boundaries of the Land of Israel (Tigay). Among the shared attributes of identity is a sense of what is pure (i.e., holy) and what is profane. People of other cultures, of other beliefs, could pollute the land and its Israelite, God-fearing inhabitants. The mere presence of an alternative to the purity of Israelite faith and culture is a threat, a refutation of the universal truth of God in the covenant with Israel. To maintain the purity of the faithful demands the eradication of the cultural foreigner, the blasphemous "other," from the midst of the nation (Milgrom 1991: 43).

The command to eradicate the impure occupants of the Land of Israel once it is conquered is found in the Torah. Its implementation in the Book of Joshua describes how this heir of Moses proceeds to vanquish all the inhabitants of the land:

> For it was the Lord himself who hardened their hearts to wage war against Israel, so that he might destroy them totally, exterminating them without mercy, as the Lord had commanded Moses. . . . So Joshua took the entire land, just as the Lord had directed Moses, and he gave it as an inheritance to Israel according to their tribal divisions.
>
> *(Joshua 11: 20–23)*

This biblical view is that the Canaanite inhabitants had no right to the land and were judged by God to be worthy of death to purify the uncleanness of the land promised by God to the true owner, Israel. Foreigners, with their heretical influence, were banned from the land Israel occupied. In the ongoing conflict in Israel today, there is no shortage of voices who cite this understanding of the Bible to justify expelling those who are not

Jewish, the "other" who threatens Jewish supremacy in the land God promised.

The ideological precursor that justifies the conquest can be found in Numbers 25:7 when a prince of Israel, during the wandering from Egypt, flagrantly has sex with a Midianite (non-Israelite) woman at the entry to the sacred sanctuary. The sin is not just public sex but the contamination, the impurity, that dangerously seduces Israelites. The couple are speared to death as blasphemers, but the zealot priest Pinchas, who murders them, is honored by God with a covenant of peace. The medieval commentator Rashi even added, if a man "commits harlotry with an Aramean woman, zealous people have the right to strike him down" (Rashi). The danger of spiritual dilution, of damaging the covenant between God and Israel, is always present anywhere in the world. But the obligation to keep the Land of Israel, the sacred land bequeathed by God to Israel to be a holy people, a kingdom of priests, is paramount. Allowing non-Israelites a presence in the Holy Land could cause God to abandon the Israelites and flee the foreign-inspired contamination of a polluted temple.

Yet, as the biblical story unfolds, once the Israelites settle in the Land of Israel, many non-Israelite tribes remain, often under Israelite rule. They become military officers for King David and builders for King Solomon. They marry Israelites, as did Ruth the Moabite, who becomes the ancestor of David and Solomon. Moreover, we know from the *Book of Ruth* that non-Israelites are included in the laws that require leaving the crop-producing edges of the field and all produce that falls to the ground to the poor as commanded in Deuteronomy. The moral imperative to care for the stranger is clear and will be written into law by rabbis over the millennia.

That said, the mandate to maintain Israelite, hence Jewish, purity in the consecrated Land of Israel is not merely an ancient command. These biblical exhortations of purity translate into law in the State of Israel. For example, in Israel, a Jew cannot legally marry a non-Jew. Likewise, on 10 March 2022, to limit the dangers of Jewish diminution in the Holy Land, Israel's parliament passed a law denying naturalization to Palestinians from the occupied West Bank or Gaza married to Israeli Palestinian citizens, forcing thousands of Palestinian families to either emigrate or live apart. Thus, what the tradition sees as polluting the purity of the covenanted Land of Israel is applied to contemporary secular, albeit religiously influenced, policy.

Jewish debates over who can live in the Land of Israel, who can become a citizen, and whose presence is proscribed continue long after the Jewish Bible is completed. Deep into medieval times, scholars disagreed over how Jews should engage non-Jews whether in Israel or abroad. The eleventh-century scholar Maimonides is considered the greatest rabbinic thinker of the medieval period, born in Spain, who became a physician to the vizier of Egypt. Considered a moderate exponent of Jewish law, his views on Gentiles are complicated. In the Mishnah Torah, his masterful compendium of Jewish law, he writes (*Sefer Nezikim*, Chapter 4):

> With regard to a gentile idolater with whom we are not at war, a shepherd of small livestock, and the like, by contrast, we should not try to cause their deaths. It is, however, forbidden to save their lives if their lives are threatened. For example, if such a person fell into the sea, one should not rescue him. Leviticus 19:16 states: "Do not stand idly by while your brother's blood is at stake." This does not apply with regard to such individuals, because they are not "your brothers."

The great thirteenth-century scholar Ramban, also known as Nachmanides, was the medieval spokesperson for the sanctity of the Land of Israel. In response to the scriptural claim that the whole world belongs to God, he explained that Israel is the nub of the world, the Holy One's private estate, bequeathed only to the people who proclaim the unity of God's name, God's darling seed, the Jewish people (Newman 1968: 21). The commandment concerning Israel, he explained, is twofold: conquest and occupation.

This read of the tradition can be heard with even more clarity in the words of later rabbis who lived under Christian rule in Europe. Some scholars claimed that any good deeds performed by Gentiles are done for ulterior motives and cannot possibly reflect essential goodness. Therefore, strangers who are not authentically Jewish are only a source of pollution for the Jewish people and the Holy Land of Israel (Bendarsh 2019). Jewish identity is highly communitarian, with bonds that define membership and resist inclusion into the community. Unlike many other faiths, Judaism has been almost exclusively non-proselytizing, valuing tribal ties over expansion. No doubt this theological stance has impacted how best to sustain the purity of God's people, limiting who could reside in the sacred Land of Israel (Elcott 2021: 139–40).

Yet these voices of exclusion are not the only voices, either in the past or in the present. The biblical view of the *ger* (the stranger who is resident in the Land of Israel) made clear that, since there is no such thing as conversion in the Bible for a resident stranger, "the *ger* is completely equivalent to the Israelite in civil law" (Milgrom 1991: 1417). The sages of the Talmud were aware that migration is to be expected when people suffer: "One who has not made good in one place and fails to move and try his luck in some other place has only oneself to complain about" (Babylonian Talmud, Bava Metzia 75b). One need not continue to reside in a land where there is no relief from suffering, whether from violence or from poverty. In the Mishnah, rabbinic conversations compiled over a few hundred years and codified in the third century in the Land of Israel, the rabbis who authored this compilation brought alive and expanded the biblical commandments of Deuteronomy that protect the non-Israelite. They demanded that Jews care for the stranger, providing food, clothing, shelter, and even burying the Gentile (including pagan) dead (aware that burial is often a sacramental and selfless act):

> The poor of the heathens are not prevented from gathering the left over and forgotten sheaves of grain as well as the corners of the field – all this in the interest of peace. Our rabbis have taught: We support the poor of the heathen along with the poor of Israel, we visit the sick of the heathen along with the sick of Israel and bury the poor of the heathen along with the poor of Israel, in the interests of peace.
>
> *(Babylonian Talmud, Gittin 61a)*

Maimonides reiterated this Talmudic command of caring for the stranger in seeming contradiction to his statement cited above. He states that caring for the stranger – feeding, healing, and burying the heathen – is a supernal ethical command because it must be done "for the sake of peace" (Maimonides, M. Hilchot Matanot Aniyim, 7:7).

The same Nachmanides who seemed to call for the eradication of Gentiles commented compassionately on the commandment in Exodus 22:20 to care for the stranger:

> In my opinion, [God] is saying, do not oppress a stranger or wrong him [by] thinking that there is no one to save him from your hand, because you know that you were strangers in the Land of Egypt. But I saw the oppression that the Egyptians put to you and I brought vengeance upon them because I see the tears of the oppressed who have no comforter while the hand of the oppressors has power. . . . You know that every stranger is disheartened and sighs and cries out, with eyes directed toward God. And God will have mercy on [the stranger] just as God had mercy on you.

The narrative tradition also provides strong support for the obligation of Jews to welcome the stranger even beyond the Mishnah's command to care for the poor. As one contemporary rabbinic commentator notes:

> Jewish tradition reminds us not to become like the land of Sodom, the paradigmatic evil society described in the Book of Genesis, which is said to have been cruel to strangers in its midst. "They issued a proclamation in Sodom saying, 'Everyone who strengthens the hand of the poor and the needy and the stranger with a loaf of bread shall be burnt by fire'" (Pirke D'Rebbe Eliezer). The foremost crime of Sodom was that they did not sustain the needs of the stranger passing through their lands.
> *(Yanklowitz n.d.)*

Israel Addresses Who Is Authentic

This debate over the place of Gentiles within the Jewish sphere spans millennia. It is summarized well by a contemporary Israeli rabbi:

> We have seen two very different conceptions of the difference between Jews and gentiles. The *Sefer HaKuzari* and the (Hassidic) *Tanya* see an essential difference between Jew and gentile,

expressed as qualitative superiority by the *Kuzari* and as the contrast between good and evil by the *Tanya*. The Rambam, whose view resonates with contemporary sensibilities, understood that all human beings are essentially alike and that the exalted nature of the Jewish soul results from the educational influence of Torah and *mitzvot*. This dispute affects the way we view and relate to gentiles, converts, and renegade Jews. We concluded with Rav Kook's observation that even if we take the perspective of essential Jewish superiority, the conclusion should not be that the gentiles exist only to serve the Jews, but rather that the Jews were chosen in order to bring Godliness and spirituality to the entire human race.

(Bendarsh 2019)

With the establishment of the State of Israel, the theoretical and homiletic statements of powerless rabbis living under Christian or Muslim rule shifted dramatically. Now, rabbis were empowered to render decisions that would have a direct impact on the laws and policies of the nation. Here, we see how ancient and medieval texts could be used to shape Jewish views on the place of non-Jews in the State of Israel. The Declaration of Independence of the State of Israel (which we will cite in the Case Study chapter) states unequivocally that Israel is open to all peoples and ensures core civil rights and freedoms. It was endorsed by the entire assembly including Orthodox Jews and rabbis. That promise remains, even though the reality is more complex.

On one side, you can hear the panic over identity, over the purity of the Jewish people. For example, Rabbi Yitzhak Yosef, the Sephardic Chief Rabbi of Israel, in a 2016 homily, explained the concession that allows non-Jews to live in Israel. He claimed that if only the Messiah had arrived, Jews would have had the power to expel them all, exactly as God commanded. Instead, Gentiles who accept the Noahide laws – a basic moral code that includes prohibitions on denying the existence of God, blasphemy, murder, illicit sexual relations, theft, and eating from a live animal, as well as a requirement to instate a legal system – could remain solely because they would fulfill roles reserved for Gentiles in the service of Jews (Times of Israel 2016).

To be clear, this is not Israeli law but the pronouncements of the Chief Rabbi who is a government official. But, given the influence of the Chief Rabbi, one cannot dismiss such views as fringe statements.

These views do not reflect the position of many Jews in Israel, perhaps even the majority, who abhor what they see as racist views imposed by some rabbis and government officials. As Israeli leader Tomer Persico explains:

> More than posing a threat, violent at times, to the lives and ways of life of other Jews in Israel, these fundamentalist Jewish groups twist the Jewish tradition into an abominable chimera, mixing biblical literalism, ethno-nationalism, and theological obsessions similar to those of American evangelical Christians, morphing Judaism into a toxic creed that is unrecognizable and unapproachable by the vast majority of living Jews.

He then adds:

> As such, they pose a threat not only to the future of Israel as a democracy, but also to the character and moral stature of Judaism itself. For these groups to become the face of Judaism in Israel, or even one of its dominant expressions, would be a historically consequential event with devastating repercussions.
> *(Persico 2024)*

That said, as we shall see in the Case Study chapter, the view that non-Jews are a danger to the purity of Israel perhaps reflects the dominant view of the governing leaders of the State of Israel even as the opposition to this government streams into the streets in protest (Pfeffer 2022).

Policies of exclusion may not be the last word, as Jewish tradition is used to critique those calling for the expulsion of non-Jews. A clear statement about Israeli policy came from Maj. Gen. Yehuda Fuchs, the outgoing chief of Israel's Central Command, which is responsible for the country's military forces in the West Bank. He decries the extremist minority of violent settlers who sow fear among Palestinians, forcing them to flee their homes. "I took seriously every stone and bottle that was thrown, and

I saw myself responsible for every person injured in body or soul. Sometimes I failed. I will carry the price of their blood with me forever." In describing the attempts to force Palestinians off the land, he added, "That, to me, is not Judaism," he said. "At least not what I was raised on in my father's and mother's home. That is not the way of the Torah" (Harel 2024).

Jews in the Diaspora

For the many centuries during which the Jews lived in the diaspora, they were in no position to determine state policy even if, on a personal level, Jews cared for non-Jews. Instead, Jews often were the chattel of the ruler and depended on protection and support. Powerless to effect change, rabbis and other Jewish leaders did not address issues outside their own community. Where there was interaction with outsiders, Jews were well aware of their vulnerability. In these circumstances, maintaining a policy that did not restrict caring solely to Jews was both religiously sanctioned and politically wise.

As Jews were integrated into European and North American societies, they were no longer isolated. Jews were members of a faith community and maintained the identity of peoplehood. Yet they also became citizens and patriots of a particular nation. Jewish interaction with others and a sense of shared destiny as citizens of the nation fostered ever more engagement. This complex identity offered a new perspective on engaging the "other" as a fellow citizen.

As a minority member of the nation, supporting human and civil rights was certainly a means of self-preservation. As with other faiths that experienced the Enlightenment and modernity, caring for the "other" soon became ingrained in Jewish values. In 1776, Hayim Solomon helped to underwrite the American Revolution in the name of the new notion of citizen democracy. Following the French Revolution, in response to Napoleon's request for clarification as to Jewish commitment to revolutionary France, Jewish notables proudly proclaimed their fealty to France, describing how French Jewish soldiers proudly fought and killed British Jewish soldiers in the name of the French Republic

(Elcott). As Jews were gradually allowed to become citizens, they often also became passionate defenders of their country and fellow citizens.

A most intriguing debate takes place in the diaspora over whether a Jewish doctor can break the Sabbath by driving to or working in a hospital to save a non-Jew. The acclaimed Halakhic rigorously Orthodox jurist Rabbi Moshe Feinstein (1895–1986) stated that "A refusal to treat a non-Jew on the Sabbath would be totally unacceptable" (Feinstein 1959). This could be seen as a halakhic legal mandate by one of the most important Jewish jurists. Yes, one could also read this as a concession to living in an overwhelmingly non-Jewish society, making a refusal to care for a non-Jew socially unacceptable. Yet there is no question that he also grounded his decision in the value of human life and that his non-Jewish neighbors must be cared for. In the language of both Jewish law and the prophetic tradition, "all human beings are created in God's image," the words taken directly from the first chapter of Genesis. Feinstein is following the Rabbinic tradition (Mishnah Sanhedrin 4:5) that each human life is precious, unique, and worthy. The implication is clear. We can see in this a pragmatic and spiritual merger; what is right to do also protects the vulnerable people in society.

In the modern period, Jewish values of doing what is just and right challenge legal Halakhic decisions. "The Mishnah Berurah" of Israel Meir Kagan (1838–1933), known as the Hafetz Hayyim, opposed the behavior of Jewish doctors who did not distinguish between Jews and non-Jews. He failed to convince and ended up complaining that "even the most religious do not take any heed whatsoever of this law, for they work on the Sabbath and travel significant distances to treat a non-Jew, and they grind medicine with their own hands" (Orekh Hayyim 330). Jewish law (behavioral norms) was overridden by what the community perceived as higher spiritual values, at least in the diaspora where Rabbi Kagan lived.

The tension between a setting where a Jewish majority controls society and the law and one where Jews must adjust to being a scrutinized minority and part of a shared national culture is obvious. Jews hoping to live in harmony in a society with neighbors, friends, and family who are not Jewish have a very different view of obligation and responsibility to non-Jews than those living in an exclusive Jewish state or community.

Today, Jews are coworkers and neighbors of people of different faiths and ethnicities. Jews have become presidents and prime ministers of nations in which they are a minority. They are researchers and advocates of policies that may have nothing to do directly with Judaism or the fate of Jews. Jewish identity in the contemporary period of nation-states in which Jews are a religious and ethnic minority is, therefore, much more complex with values and norms adapting to an integrated world.

In the contemporary period, caring for their fellow non-Jewish citizens has become a virtue, an act of civic engagement, of deeply Jewish meaning as well as pragmatic self-preservation. Caring for the stranger, for the suffering of others, has been invoked as part of the diaspora Jewish commitment to partner with God in *Tikkun Olam,* an obligation to repair a broken, suffering world (Elcott). This can be read in the mission and vision statements of synagogues, rabbinic associations, and Jewish organizations, such as the Hebrew Immigrant Aid Society (HIAS) or the American Jewish World Service, the Religious Action Center, and the National Association of Jewish Women, who live out this commitment to be God's partner in healing those who are suffering and repairing the inequities of the modern world. It is seen in the surveys of Jews in the United States who value social justice and ethical living, along with remembering the Holocaust, as the highest Jewish virtues (Pew Research Center 2020).

Immigration, Jewish Purity, and Jewish Caring for the Stranger

In the twenty-first century, as the Introduction states, immigration has become a more pressing international issue. War, climate change, hunger, and economic collapse have sent over 120 million people from their homes. Jewish values, whether a demand for purity in the Land of Israel or determining policy based on the Jewish diaspora refugee experience, must speak to the challenge of immigration.

To be serious actors effecting policy is new to Judaism, a product of only the last few hundred years. In the past, Jewish law obligated its adherents to redeem the captive if the person captured was Jewish (Talmud Baba Batra 8:3). There was no law or principle to redeem refugees who were not Jews and no real opportunity to engage. Radical change in the place of Jews in the world offers new theological terrain. In the case of immigration, Jewish attitudes concerning asylum for non-Jewish refugees fleeing oppression have come into focus for reasons beyond their new roles as patriotic citizens and government officials.

World War II and the destruction of European Jewry have become a central and commanding memory for Jews. Opposition to immigration for Jews fleeing the Nazi terror focused specifically on the danger of adding Jews to America. When Congress debated a bill in 1939 to bring 20,000 Jewish children from Europe to America, opposition was fierce. For example, Francis Kinnicutt of Fair Hills, New Jersey, president of the Allied Patriotic Society, which included societies like the Sons of the Revolution and Daughters of the Revolution, testified, "If the bill were enacted into law, the additional immigration permitted by it would be for the most part of the Jewish race." (Israel 2023) The bill ultimately failed to add any children beyond the existing limited quotas. Millions died, unable to find sanctuary. Beyond biblical or rabbinic texts, the painful experiences of Jews in the diaspora are ingrained in memory. History speaks powerfully. Reference to the failure to allow asylum to Jews facing genocide remains at the core of Jewish political support in the United States for comprehensive immigration reform.

The Jewish community in the United States, the largest diaspora Jewish community with thousands of synagogues, social justice organizations, scholars, and rabbis, has an important perspective on the immigration debate. Because the memory of rejection that led to the loss of millions of European Jews looms large, the mandate to care for your neighbor has expanded to include not only the circle of fellow citizens but also others who may be endangered around the world as Jews were endangered in World War II. For the majority of Jews in the United States, the iconic phrase "Never Again" is applied to mean that no people, no human beings, should suffer isolation and abandonment as Jews did during the Holocaust. Add to this strong American Jewish commitment to *Tikkun Olam,* that Jews must partner with God in repairing the world, and you see the emergence of a uniquely modern Jewish theology of engagement in the world.

The Jewish immigrants that ultimately came to these shores adopted core American values and civic responsibilities. For a few, this meant adopting the resentments of some segments of America against immigrants. Yet these voices reflect a very limited minority. The memory of past wanderings and oppression and the activist role of citizens apply this emergent contemporary theology to welcome the stranger as part of the American Jewish effort to repair the world. As Rabbi Stephanie Crawley explains when voicing support for positive and welcoming immigration reform:

> Often when we hear from religious leaders in America, we hear things to the right. It's important to give a message from where I sit, which I see as the Jewish moral voice and the voice of Torah. Unless our leaders hear from what we believe is a Jewish and theological underpinning of what our ethics and morals are, we will always lose the religious voice to other religions and more conservative voices.
>
> *(Samuel 2024)*

As we have shown, Jewish theological thinking evolved in the diaspora in its engagement with the world. Supporting a positive and welcoming immigration policy is rooted in core values based on scripture and history as well as a pragmatic stance to be good citizens. It speaks powerfully to the overwhelming majority of American Jews. Every Passover, Jews read from the Haggadah, the text central to the Jewish story: "In every generation, each person is required to see themselves as if they personally left Egypt." This verse is cited often as the source of Jewish support for immigration reform and the acceptance of asylum seekers and refugees. Thus, the Jewish identity of American Jews that derives from a shared historical experience as immigrants fueled by ancient religious texts, norms, and values unites the overwhelming majority of American Jews to support a generous immigration reform.

References

Bendarsh, Asaf. (2019). "Adapted by Leora Bednarsh". *Mussar and Faith*. Viewed from: www.etzion.org.il/en/philosophy/issues-jewish-thought/issues-mussar-and-faith/jews-and-gentiles [Date accessed: 24 October 2024].

Elcott, David. (1995). *A Sacred Journey: The Jewish Quest for a Perfect World*, (Pp. 63–6). New York: Roman and Littlefield.

Elcott, David. (2021). *Faith, Nationalism and the Future of Liberal Democracy*. Bloomington: Notre Dame Press.

Farbiaz, Rachel. "Treatment of the Stranger, Commentary on Parashat Vaetchanan, My Jewish Learning". Viewed from: www.myjewishlearning.com/article/treatment-of-the-stranger/ [Date accessed: 23 October 2024].

Feinstein, M. (1959). *Igrot Moshe, Orah Hayyim 4:79*, commentary on Bible text.

Firetone, R. (n.d.). "The Commandment to Love and Help the Stranger, Reform Judaism". Viewed from: https://reformjudaism.org/learning/torah-study/torah-commentary/commandment-love-and-help-stranger [Date accessed: 23 October 2024].

Haidt, J. (2012). *The Righteous Mind*. New York: Pantheon.

Harel, Amos. (2024). "In His Retirement Speech, Israel's Top Officer in the West Bank Revealed the Hidden Truth". Viewed from: www.haaretz.com/israel-news/2024-07-09/ty-article/.premium/in-his-retirement-speech-israels-top-officer-in-the-west-bank-revealed-the-hidden-truth/00000190-93fc-d1c5-a1d6-bbfc58e20000 [Date accessed: 23 October 2024].

Herkanus, Eliezer Ben. (2008). *Pirke D'Rebbe Eliezer 25*. India: Varda.

Israel, Steve. (2023). "As Yom Kippur Approaches, the Legacy of America's Treatment of Jewish Refugees Must Be a Call to Action". *Viewed in: The Forward*. Viewed from: https://forward.com/opinion/561774/yom-kippur-migrants-jewish- [Date accessed: 23 October 2024].

Kagan, Y. *Orekh Hayyim 330*, commentary on Bible text. Bnei Brak: Sefarati.

Maimonides, M. (1988). *Hilchot Matanot Aniyim ("Gifts to the Poor") 7:7*. Jerusalem: Ch. Vageshel.

Milgrom, Jacob. (1991). *Leviticus*, Vol. 1. *Anchor Bible*. New York: Doubleday.

Nachmanides, M. Viewed from: www.sefaria.org/Ramban_on_Exodus.22.20?lang=bi

Newman, A. (1968). "Tradition: Volume 10". Summer. Viewed from: www.jstor.org/stable/23256370 [Date accessed: 23 October 2024].

Persico, T. (2024). "Sources". Viewed from: www.sourcesjournal.org/articles/a-natural-act-of-vengeance-settler-violence-and-two-types-of-jewish-fundamentalism [Date accessed: 24 October 2024].

Pew Research Center. (2020). Viewed from: www.pewresearch.org/religion/2021/05/11/jewish-americans-in-2020/

Pfeffer, Anshel. (2022). "Netanyahu's New Ministers". Viewed from: www.nytimes.com/2022/12/30/opinion/netanyahus-new-ministers-have-very-strict-ideas-about-who-is-a-jew.html [Date accessed: 24 October 2024].

Rashi. 1971. *Bamidbar, 25:7*. New York: Friedman.

Samuel, Ben. (2024). "Make America Great Again". Viewed from: www.haaretz.com/us-news/2024-07-02/ty-article-magazine/.premium/make-america-greet-again-why-immigration-matters-for-u-s-jewish-voters-this-november/00000190-726b-d3a4-a592-7e7bb5000000 [Date accessed: 24 October 2024].

Tigay, J. (1998). *Deuteronomy, The JPS Commentary*, (P. 470). Philadelphia: JPS.

Times of Israel Staff. (2016). "Chief Rabbi: Non-Jews Shouldn't Be Allowed to Live in Israel". Viewed from: www.timesofisrael.com/chief-rabbi-non-jews-shouldnt-be-allowed-to-live-in-israel/ [Date accessed: 24 October 2024].

Yanklowitz, Shmuly. (n.d.). "Judaism and Immigration". Viewed from: www.myjewishlearning.com/article/judaism-and-immigration/ [Date accessed: 24 October 2024].

2
CHRISTIANITY AND IMMIGRATION POLICY

Several disputed questions in Christianity converge on immigration policy: the relationship between church and state, the use of political power, one's relative duty to family versus to all humanity, and how the Bible can be interpreted for present-day ethical concerns. Rather than present a top-down theological argument that would fail to speak on behalf of all Christians, this chapter begins with what all Christians hold in common before presenting the diverse Christian attitudes to immigration along with the theological arguments that support them. Even then, it is out of scope to encompass all forms of global Christianity. It will discuss two in particular: (1) Christianity in Europe, with a special focus on the history of Catholic immigration policy up to the present day, and (2) Evangelicalism in America, with a special focus on how the Bible has been invoked in immigration debates. It will also have a brief note on the Orthodox Church.

This chapter builds on the two understandings of religion given in the Introduction: (1) communal identity and (2) commitment to beliefs/practices. These are not mutually exclusive categories: people can understand their faith in both ways. The argument of this chapter is twofold. First, it contends that where Christianity is understood primarily as a national identity, immigration policies tend to be hostile to foreigners from other religious traditions. Such hostility is due to attempts to preserve as much overlap as possible between religious affiliation and national identity. Second, this chapter argues that those who understand their Christianity primarily as a commitment to a set of beliefs and

DOI: 10.4324/9781032645209-3

practices tend to see in Christian teaching an injunction to welcome and protect the stranger and have acted on that teaching in numerous ways.

Exceptions abound. As we shall see, theological arguments for border restriction have been made by people deeply committed to the tenets and practices of their faith. Yet, even in these cases, this chapter suggests that such arguments are rooted in a conception of Christianity that is intertwined with national or European identity.

As the Introduction also notes, it would be simplistic to blame or praise a religion for everything its members do. Much of what Christians do is simply because they are human: eating, sleeping, being anxious about the future, seeking comfort and security, protecting their own, and fearing the other. It may be that in some cases, the true cause of pro- or anti-immigration sentiments is a more primordial impulse to which Christianity only provides superficial clothing. This chapter does not attempt to judge; it presents the arguments Christians make for their positions, leaving an assessment of their authenticity to the reader.

Basic Christian Principles

Christians have argued for a wide range of immigration policies, from radical exclusiveness to open borders. Yet, amidst this diversity of views, the following five principles remain constant across all Christian traditions.

First, Christianity teaches that all human beings are made in God's image, regardless of race, ethnicity, gender, nationality, political or religious affiliation, beliefs, or history (Genesis 1:27). Nothing that a human being does can destroy this stamp of the divine in them. The meaning of *imago Dei* has been interpreted in many ways (see Peppiatt 2022), but a common thread that runs throughout is that it endows every human individual with a dignity that exceeds plants, animals, and inanimate objects. Simply by being a human being they warrant respect and recognition. In early modernity some Dominican friars built on the doctrine of *imago Dei* to develop the discourse of universal human rights (Hollenbach, SJ 2019).

Second, Christianity commands compassion for, and solidarity with, the poor and marginalized of all kinds – mentally or physically disabled, oppressed, discriminated against, elderly, homeless, unborn, or any other kind of disadvantage, including migrants and especially forced migrants. This solidarity should take the form of practical support and provision, as well as political action toward a just society. It is unconditional, meaning it does not ask the question of whether or not people "deserve" it – rather, it is based on the abovementioned *imago Dei*. The list of Bible passages on this topic would be too long to give. In the twentieth century, it was given the appellation "God's preferential option for the poor" by the influential Liberation Theology movement.

Third, Christianity teaches that the Christian's citizenship is in heaven and any earthly citizenship is subordinate to it (Philippians 3:20). This has several consequences, two of which are relevant here. First, it means that a Christian's primary loyalty is to God above any earthly government or authority. Second, it means that Christians are not to see themselves as ultimately belonging to any earthly nationality, ethnicity, or people group. Such belonging is secondary to membership in the church.

Fourth, Christianity commands submission to earthly rulers and authorities except where such submission would explicitly violate their duty to God (Romans 13 – this will be discussed in more depth below). Christians are not to willfully ignore their nation's laws or undermine national stability simply out of personal preference or whim. Only in extreme circumstances, such as those brought about by the Nazi regime in the twentieth century, are Christians permitted – even required – to engage in civil disobedience.

Fifth and finally, the vast majority of Christians hold to some version of the *ordo amoris* ("order of loves"), according to which an individual's duty to their immediate family is greater than their duty to all of humanity. This view normally envisions responsibility in concentric circles, with one's closest kin in the center and a stranger on the other side of the world at the periphery. This fifth principle was the focus of a prominent debate on X (née Twitter), between US Vice President J.D. Vance and political commentator Rory Stewart, regarding the US government's actions under the 2025 Trump administration. A brief synopsis of these events and arguments will be treated in the final chapter of this book. Here, we shall outline the principle as it appears in its original sources, St. Augustine of Hippo and St. Thomas Aquinas. Augustine writes:

> All men are to be loved equally. But since you cannot do good to all, you are to pay special regard to those who, by the accidents of time, or place, or circumstance, are brought into closer connection with you.
>
> *(Augustine of Hippo 1887: I.28)*

This "closer connection" need not be understood only as referring to kinship, ethnicity, or citizenship but can mean someone in need who is geographically close. In other words, I have a greater responsibility to those in need who are in my neighborhood, whether family members or foreigners, than to those far away.

Aquinas seeks to remove ambiguity by formalizing the principle more precisely. He writes:

> We ought in preference to bestow on each one such benefits as pertain to the matter in which, speaking simply, he is most closely connected with us. And yet this may vary according to the various requirements of time, place, or matter in hand: because in certain cases one ought, for instance, to succor a stranger, in extreme necessity, rather than one's own father, if he is not in such urgent need.
>
> The case may occur, however, that one ought rather to invite strangers, on account of their greater want. For it must be understood that, other things being equal, one ought to succor those rather who are most closely connected with us. And if of two, one be more closely connected, and the other in greater want, it is not possible to decide, by any general rule, which of them we ought to help rather than the other, since there are various degrees of want as well as of connection: and the matter requires the judgment of a prudent man.
>
> *(Aquinas 1911: Summa Theologiae II-II.Q31.A3.C&Rep1)*

The founders of the *ordo amoris* tradition are therefore clear that this principle ought not to serve as an excuse to ignore disadvantaged strangers on the basis of their lower priority compared to family members.

These five principles can be seen to varying degrees across all forms and types of Christianity. They represent the foundations upon which any Christian immigration policy is built. Yet, as we shall see, they are interpreted and weighed differently, not only by each Christian tradition but also within each tradition as conflicting forces seek to determine how they apply to the contemporary scene. Let us begin by surveying these conflicts in the continent that has traditionally been called "Christian" and which, in the views of many, remains so.

Christians in Europe: Past and Present

Setting the Scene: Demographic Trends

> "European values" have been invoked both to support refugees and migrants and to attack them.
> *(Goździak & Main 2020: 3)*

The Europe of today presents us with a complex mix of Christian attitudes to immigration. Throughout the continent, populist politicians have appealed to the preservation of "European values" or "Christian values" (these are seen as the same thing) as a reason to keep Muslims out, drawing on a centuries-long history of conflict between Christianity and Islam around European territories. At the same time, many church leaders have spoken out in favor of immigrant welcome and criticized the harsh treatment of immigrants by their government. The layperson finds himself/herself caught between voices on the right and the left, both claiming to speak on behalf of Christian Europe.

What follows is not a comprehensive survey of Christian views in Europe. It is better seen as a series of vignettes that show the diversity of ways Christianity is being invoked, both in support of immigrant welcome and as a reason to restrict borders. A more detailed analysis of Germany and Hungary will be done in a later chapter.

Poland and the Czech Republic

The hostility toward Muslim immigrants among Polish Catholics offers a sharp contrast to the warm welcome of Muslims by Czech Catholics. This supports the notion that attitudes to immigration become increasingly negative as religious identity becomes tied to national identity, while the more people take seriously the doctrinal and ethical elements of Christianity, the more likely they are to be welcoming to strangers.

Poland has the reputation of being one of the most religious nations in Europe and one of the most hostile to immigration. However, both of these perceptions need qualification. While 86% of the Polish population are Catholic, only 28% attend weekly mass (Coppen 2023). In short, "The majority of Poles seem to declare their affiliation to the Church but do not participate in its rituals" (Wilczyńska & Wilczyński 2020: 92–3).

Nor is Poland against all kinds of immigration but only immigration from Muslim-majority countries. The Polish government has welcomed huge numbers of Ukrainian refugees. This is because, as Goździak and Suter (2020: 288) point out, "Ukrainians are perceived by the Polish government as culturally close to Poles and therefore easier to integrate." The hostility to Muslim refugees cannot be on the basis of their racial or ethnic identity since Poland has been negotiating a bilateral agreement with the Philippines to accept thousands of Filipino workers to fill a gap in their labor population. Since "80% of Filipinos are Catholic" (Mazurczak 2018), it seems clear that Poland's readiness to welcome Filipinos is, as with Ukrainians, due to their shared Christian identity. No matter your language or skin color, if you are Christian, then you are welcome in Poland. If you are Muslim, then you are not welcome.

Polish politicians give two reasons for keeping Muslims out. The first is security. Muslims are perceived as a dangerous threat, liable to be radicalized and become terrorists. In 2016, following the influx of Syrian refugees into Europe, the prime minister announced that "Poland would not accept any refugees under the plan. Explaining this decision, the government spokesman Rafal Bochenek pointed to the security of the member state citizens"

(Krotofil & Motak 2018: 63). In a famous TV interview, Polish MP Dominik Tarczynski said that while Poland had accepted two million "peaceful Ukrainians," it would "not receive even one Muslim." He went on to justify this by saying, "this is why Poland is so safe. This is the reason why we have not even one terrorist attack" (In Context 2022). In the same interview, he referred to "Muslim illegal immigrants," appearing to conflate all three categories – refugee, Muslim, and illegal immigrant – as if they were the same thing. Although Tarczynski has insisted that Poland's stance has "nothing to do with religion. It has nothing to do with Islamophobia. It's all about safety" (The Newsmakers 2019); when one interviewer responded, "not all Muslims are terrorists," he replied (correcting himself halfway through the sentence) "but all terrorists – most terrorists are Muslims" (Al Jazeera 2019: 8:18).

The second reason given for keeping Muslims out of Poland is to preserve Christian culture and cultural homogeneity. For example, Tarczynski says that "for me, multicultural society – it's not a value" (Al Jazeera 2019: 5:42). Instead, "Christian culture, Roman law, Greek philosophers, these are the virtues for us" (Al Jazeera 2019: 6:04). He did not provide any concrete examples of what virtues are espoused by "Christian culture" and whether welcoming of strangers, especially those forced to flee their homes, might be among them. Nor did he seem aware that Greek philosophers are a shared heritage of Christianity and Islam, and Christianity discovered Aristotle from Islamic scholars in the Middle Ages. In other words, he showed a remarkable absence of theological and historical knowledge despite basing his position on the differences between Christianity and Islam.

However, the politicians' lack of theological acuity is not corrected by those with greater theological training. The majority of Polish priests and bishops have supported their government's anti-refugee stance. Since 2015, "Church leaders, as well as ordinary members of the Catholic Church in Poland, began using the figure of a Muslim pretending to be a refugee as a synonym of a threat to the Catholic identity of the country" (Wilczyńska & Wilczyński 2020: 96). A minority of clergy have spoken out against this trend and instead stood alongside Pope Francis in calling for greater welcome of refugees, but their voices were drowned out by the majority.

Yet, in the Czech Republic, Catholics have a more positive attitude toward Muslim immigrants. To explain this striking difference, Bell and Strabac (2020) point to the different role Catholicism plays in both countries. In Poland, religious identity is tightly bound up with national identity and has been for decades, to the point where it is commonly understood that "to be a Pole means to be a Catholic" (Krotofil & Motak 2018: 75). Two recent surveys have revealed that "64% of Poles indicated that religion is a key component of national identity" and "54% of respondents agreed that Polish identity is defined by being Roman Catholic" (Górak-Sosnowska & Pachocka 2019: 228). Poles interviewed by Jaskulowski (2019: 60) said that

> Catholicism is so intertwined with Polish culture that it has also stamped its mark on non-believers. [Interviewees] also pointed to a common system of values; however, they either did not specify these values in detail or merely referred to vague stereotypes such as the love of freedom.

So if we ask why Catholicism is so important in Poland, the answer for many seems to have little to do with Catholic theology or practice, but that Catholic identity is a marker of Polishness. This is a very clear example of religious identity being absorbed into national identity to the point where religion's only purpose is to contribute to national identity.

For Czech Catholics, by contrast, their faith is a commitment to a set of beliefs and a way of life, which is unequivocally compassionate and welcoming. Bell and Strabac summarize:

> To understand the role of religion in terms of ethnic prejudice one needs to understand what it is that motivates individuals to be religious. Belonging to a religion because it gives comfort and power indicates that it creates a feeling of being a member of an in-group. . . . But if an individual belongs to a religion because of the values of the religion, that individual will more likely be less prejudiced and a more tolerant person. . . . The

Catholic faith is very much linked to the Polish identity, while in the Czech Republic a mere 10 per cent of the population regard themselves as Catholic and the remainder are primarily secular. This makes it less likely for a person to be a member of the Catholic church because of wanting to belong to a national in-group, in contrast to the case in Poland. Thus, we can assume that the majority of the members of the Catholic church in the Czech Republic are members because of the ideals and values of the religion, and not because of nationalist motives as in Poland. This may be the reason why religiosity has a positive effect in the Czech Republic.

(Bell & Strabac 2020: 141)

Sweden and the United Kingdom

In Sweden and the United Kingdom, those most committed to their Christian faith tend to be active in support of immigrants and critical of their governments' anti-immigration policies.

In Sweden, following the 2015 Syrian refugee crisis, "eight out of ten parishes had pastoral activities for and with asylum seekers and newly arrived immigrants" (Linde & Scaramuzzino 2018: 122). This welcoming response was not shared by the Swedish government, which in 2016 put forward a proposal to limit the possibilities for migrants to obtain a residence permit. The Swedish Christian Council, an umbrella organization that speaks on behalf of all Christian denominations in Sweden (Catholic, Orthodox, Lutheran, and Free Churches), strongly opposed this government proposal. In its statement, the council spoke of

> the proposal's discrepancy with many of [Christianity's] fundamental principles, including hospitality. The commentary refers to Jesus' experience of being a refugee, to the "essential values that we argue come from the gospel," and the churches' duty to protest against injustices and work for a better society for all people.
>
> *(Suter & Scaramuzzino 2020: 177–8)*

In the United Kingdom, the government has striven for decades to provide a "hostile environment" to immigrants (unless they are wealthy or highly skilled). However, these explicitly and self-avowedly hostile policies are rarely coupled with claims to defend the United Kingdom as a "Christian nation." For example, when Conservative MP Robert Jenrick combined his complaints about "unprecedented migration" with an appeal to recover "British identity," what is striking in comparison to other European nations is a complete absence of any mention of Christianity as part of that identity (Jenrick 2024).

One rare instance of the use of "Christian culture" in the United Kingdom is worth mentioning because of its starkly anti-religious origin. In April 2024, Richard Dawkins, widely considered the world's most vocal atheist, caused enormous surprise when in a TV interview he called himself a "cultural Christian." He explained that "I feel at home in the Christian ethos. I feel that we are a Christian country" (LBC 2024). Dawkins made these comments upon discovering that "Ramadan lights, rather than Easter decorations, were hung on London's Oxford Street" (Shakeshaft 2024). He went on to say that "insofar as Christianity can be considered a bulwark against Islam, I think it's a very good thing" (LBC 2024). This is an astonishing appraisal from someone who has written multiple books attacking religion in general and Christianity in particular. It is thus clear that Dawkins' sudden and unexpected warmth toward Christianity is entirely motivated by his negative view of Islam.

British Christians themselves do not talk in this way. Churches across the United Kingdom have overwhelmingly come out in support of refugees and immigrants. A huge number of faith-based refugee charities have launched, which provide all kinds of support from practical necessities and English classes to political advocacy and lobbying (Snyder 2012: 35–47). When the UK government instituted a "community sponsorship" program in which a community could sponsor the reception of a refugee, it was notable how "those organizations that have sponsored refugees are primarily faith-based (Christian) or part of the Refugees Welcome movement" (van Selm 2020: 195).

Similarly, the majority of Anglican bishops are critical of the UK government's hostile policy. The Church of England website offers guidelines and resources for parishioners on migration, emphasizing the need to show compassion and welcome for the forcibly displaced, to become educated about the terms and statistics so as to avoid being misled by false information, and to "pray for everyone to be treated in a way that is both fair and compassionate" (Church of England n.d.).

Similarly, the UK's "Rwanda Asylum Plan" evoked a strong reaction from Anglican leadership. In 2022, the UK government announced that it would begin deporting illegal immigrants and asylum seekers to Rwanda, hoping this would serve as a deterrent to prospective immigrants. The overwhelming response from the churches of England and Wales was to condemn the plan as inhumane, a violation of human rights and dignity (Church in Wales n.d.; Williams n.d.). The head of the Anglican Church of Rwanda, however, supported the plan and said Rwanda was "ready to welcome people needing a home" (Today News 2022). While this may seem like a disagreement, it shows a unified attitude of welcome from Anglican leaders relative to their region of authority. There was nonetheless a minority voice among UK Anglican clergy, who took a firm view in opposition to what they perceived as the mainstream (Biggar et al. 2022).

Italy, Germany, Austria, and France

In Italy, Germany, Austria, and France, a pattern has emerged that is confirmed by a number of studies. The politicians who are most vocal in their defense of "Christian Europe" and "Christian values" as a reason for hostile immigration policy are typically the least religiously engaged. The majority of their supporters never or seldom attend church services or read the Bible. Thus, calls to preserve "Christian culture" and "Christian values" are a veneer of nationalism. Devout Christians who are engaged with their churches, and who seek intellectual formation in Christian ways of thinking, tend to be more positive toward immigrants.

In Austria, there is a conflict between the Austrian Freedom Party's "claims to represent and 'defend' the Christian heritage of Austria in the face of an alleged 'Islamic invasion'" and the official representatives of the Catholic Church in Austria, who have strongly criticized this attitude and these claims (Wodak 2022: 214).

In Italy, anti-immigrant sentiment is strongest among those who self-identify as Catholic but who do not live particularly Catholic lives, whereas Catholics who regularly attend mass and read the Bible tend to be more welcoming of immigrants. Ladini et al. (2021: 390) offer the following explanation of these statistics:

> On the one hand, belonging to a religious community is expected to reinforce a social identity, leading to negative attitudes toward outgroups. On the other hand, religious commitment implies adhering to religious teachings which promote altruistic values, such as the acceptance of others.

Yet Catholics in Italy who are pro-immigration tend to express this support *apolitically*, not challenging the governmental policies that deport migrants and deny them housing. Ventimiglia is one example of this because, due to its location, it experienced a large buildup of refugees unable to cross into Northern Europe. During the 2015 crisis, a priest in Ventimiglia turned his church into a shelter for migrants, and the local parish became active in practical support such as providing food and clothing. A great amount of charity and aid was given to migrants in the form of practical necessities but not in the form of any attempts to change national policy (Escarcena 2020).

In Germany, there is a conflict between two conceptions of what it means to be Christian: one put forward by right-wing populists who associate Christianity with German culture, and the other championed by official church representatives who teach a more universalist ethic (Cremer 2023: 109). In fact, the loudest appeals to preserving Christian culture come from the far-right Alternative für Deutschland (AfD) party and from PEGIDA ("Patriotic Europeans Against the Islamization of the West" in translation). Yet most members of the AfD are not practicing Christians, nor are the people who vote for them. Likewise, PEGIDA uses "'Christendom' as a cultural identity marker without necessarily subscribing to 'Christianity' as a faith." Cremer suggests that these parties' use of Christianity is best understood not as "a return to religiosity in German society, but rather of the attempt of a comparatively secular – and at times openly secularist – party to employ Christianity as a secularized national identity marker against Islam" (Cremer 2023: 108).

France is similar to Germany in this regard. France's far-right party, founded by Jean-Marie Le Pen as the Front National, in 2018 renamed itself Rassemblement National (RN) under the leadership of Marine Le Pen. Since its inception, the party has been ferociously anti-immigration (Vidalon & Fuentes 2024). During the 2017 election, "the fight against immigration was the top priority among Le Pen voters, with 92 per cent of them saying 'it played a determinant role in their vote'" (Cremer 2023: 129). In recent years, their rhetoric has become more religious: the unwanted "others" are Muslims, and the "we" are Catholics. Yet, despite the RN's claims to defend France's Catholic identity, they receive little support from practicing Catholics and overt criticism from Catholic officials. In fact, according to Cremer, "high levels of religious practice have been one of the strongest statistical predictors against voting for the RN for decades, and church authorities have continuously clashed with the RN . . . on immigration" (2023: 112).

The RN does nothing to hide the fact that its use of the name "Catholic" has nothing to do with belief and practice. The former RN general secretary, for example, said "believing or not, practicing or not. . . . It's who we are – a country of Christian tradition and culture." Jean-Marie Le Pen's former deputy was clear that Catholic teachings were of no use to him, saying that he was "hostile to mass immigration" but that "members of the clergy can criticize this in good faith, given that it's a breach of the duty of Christian charity, of the universalism which is theirs, and of their moral obligation to welcome the stranger" (Cremer 2023: 145). Similarly, Marine Le Pen said she was

> "angry with the Church, because I think that it interferes in everything except what it should really be concerned with." The pope's call for European leaders to take in migrants and refugees "asks that states go against the interests of their own people."
> *(Green 2017)*

As Cremer summarizes:

> The RN, while a self-declared savior of la France Catholique, is in fact one of the most secularist parties in France. Its policies not only clash with Christian doctrine on immigration, Europe and societal questions, but are also indicative of an underlying identitarian conception of Christianity, one that seems more concerned with "Christendom" as a civilisational antidote to Islam than with Christianity as a faith.
>
> *(Cremer 2023: 154)*

Yet this hostile stance toward the religious "other," in the form of Islam, is arguably more continuous with Europe's history than any stance that is more welcoming. We find this same hostility directed toward Jews in the early modern period, from both state and church officials. Because Europe was predominantly Catholic until the Reformation, we will now turn to survey the development of Catholic immigration policy from the medieval era to the present day.

Catholic Immigration Policy in Medieval and Early Modern Europe

Migration within Europe was commonplace and unproblematic before the Reformation, partly because Europe's political structure was different from today, and the nation-state system had not yet developed. Immigration into Europe was also limited, so the question of a Christian immigration policy as such was rarely discussed, at least not by theologians. But immigration policy was nonetheless enacted, and justified, by state and church authorities. The clearest example of this is in the Church's treatment of the Jews, who represent the most visible "other" in the medieval period. For this reason, we shall focus on the treatment of Jews as an illustrative example. What we find is a story in which the Church initially stood up for the rights of Jews but then gave in to a wave of anti-Jewish aggression which was justified by theological arguments. A desire to see a complete overlap between national and religious identity lies as the implicit, unspoken background of all that goes on.

For a long time, European states encouraged Jewish immigration, but not for religious reasons. They saw Jews as a valuable asset to the economy, and many rulers created incentives to entice Jews to settle in their lands. There were, however, religious reasons for the lack of violence against Jews during this period. Until the eleventh century, the Church forbade anti-Jewish violence and taught that Jews should be allowed to live peacefully alongside Christians, a teaching that to begin with was adhered to by the people (Chazan 2023: 22).

But the populace eventually started to adhere to Church teaching on this topic less. The end of the eleventh century saw several outbreaks of violence against Jews. State and religious authorities condemned such behavior and offered the Jews protection, sometimes hiding them in churches. Poliakov writes that "almost everywhere, counts and bishops . . . attempted, sometimes even at the peril of their lives, to protect the Jews" (Poliakov 1965: 45).

The attitude then spread to Europe's political leaders. Between 1182 and 1492, Jewish communities were expelled from France, Germany, England, and Spain. Finally, religious leaders followed suit. In 1555, Pope Paul IV restricted Jews in Rome to a walled ghetto, forbade them from certain professions, and required them to wear particular clothing. Then, in 1569, Pope Pius V expelled Jews from all Papal States except those in the aforementioned ghetto and another in Ancona.

We will unpack the religious dimension to these expulsions by focusing on two in particular: (1) the 1492 expulsion from Spain because it was the largest and most well-known and (2) the 1569 expulsion from the Papal States because it was enacted by a religious authority.

The 1492 Expulsion From Spain

For decades, Spain had been the focus of a concerted effort to convert all Jews to Christianity through evangelism, incentives for converts, and disincentives for those who refused to convert. These efforts were successful enough to create a sizeable community of *conversos* who lived alongside their Jewish friends and family. However, tensions arose between the two groups, and the state authorities heard frequent reports from the Inquisition that (1) the Jews were trying to re-Judaize the *conversos*, and (2) many of the *conversos* were continuing to practice Judaism secretly. This was felt by both religious and state leadership to be a dangerous situation. King Ferdinand and Queen Isabella attempted to put an end to these Judaizing efforts by restricting Jews to their own ghettos and forbidding contact between Jews and *conversos*, but the Grand Inquisitor of Spain, a Dominican friar named Tomás de Torquemada, persuaded them that these measures were proving ineffective. He argued that the only way to prevent the spread of apostasy was to remove the Jews from Spain altogether. In a desperate bid, the Jews offered 30,000 ducats to King Ferdinand and Queen Isabella to be allowed to remain. According to legend, Ferdinand was about to accept the offer when Torquemada marched into the palace holding out a crucifix and said, "Judas sold our Savior for thirty pieces of silver, but your highnesses will sell Him for 30,000. Here He is, sell Him," and left the crucifix on the table (Hefele 1860: 309). Soon after, Ferdinand and Isabella published the expulsion edict – the text of which was based on a draft written by Torquemada (Pérez 2007: 84). In one version of the decree, they explained their decision as obedience to the Inquisition, "despite the great harm to ourselves, seeking and preferring the salvation of souls above our own profit and that of individuals" (Kamen 2014: 25). In other words, they were well aware of the economic benefits of Jews, but religion commands a higher allegiance than economic prosperity.

Religious agency, therefore, was the driving force behind the expulsion (Gerber 2012: 229). The theological reasoning appears to be as follows.

It was common in the early modern era to think of Christian Europe as Christ's body, borrowing a metaphor from the apostle Paul (cf. 1 Cor 12:12–27). Based on this metaphor, Jews were seen as "contagious aliens within the *Corpus Christianum*, and the only way to purify that Body of Christ was to expel them entirely" (Terpstra 2015: 110). We can see this language in one part of the edict:

> Whenever some grave and detestable crime is committed by some persons of a group or community, it is right that such a

college or community be dissolved and annihilated, and that the minors be punished for the elders, one for the other; and that those who pervert the good and honest living of the cities and villages, and that by contagion could injure others, be expelled from among the peoples, and even for other lighter causes that are harmful to the states, and how much more so for the greatest of the crimes, dangerous and contagious as is this one.

(Gerber 1992: 287)

The "greatest of crimes" is that of persuading Christians to apostatize. Whether they were in fact engaging in evangelistic endeavors or not (as we point out in Chapter 1, Judaism is not known for its missional dimension), what made the Jews "contagious" was their perceived success at this activity. From Torquemada's perspective, the salvation of souls was at stake. That is why he imagined the Jews as a dangerous virus that must be prevented from spreading throughout the body. The body of Christ was under attack, and the contagious influence must be wiped out before it spread any further. When the Jews offered money to the crown so that they could remain, Torquemada saw the parallel to Judas being paid to betray Jesus: it was money in exchange for the destruction of Christ's body.

The 1569 Expulsion From the Papal States

There are similarities between the Spanish and papal expulsions. A desire to convert all Jews lurks in the background of both, alongside a worry that the conversions will be in the opposite direction (Berger 1979; Stow 1977). A different biblical metaphor was in use but with the same effect: prominent Franciscans in Italy had compared Jews to yeast that threatened to sour the entire loaf of bread (cf. Gal 5:9; see Stow 1992: 258). This verse is not entirely taken out of context since Paul wrote to the Galatian Gentile Christians to warn them against practicing the Jewish law, and the metaphor expresses Paul's worry that the Judaizers would win the whole community over (de Boer 2011: 321). What makes Paul's approach different is the absence of recourse to political coercion, for which he had neither the ability nor the will.

The papal expulsion is also similar to Spain's in chronological sequence. Before being expelled, the Jews were first confined to ghettos by Paul IV in the 1555 papal bull *Cum nimis absurdum*.

According to *Cum nimis absurdum*, the Jews are natural slaves and inferiors of Christians. This is because they are guilty of having killed Christ, and this guilt "has consigned them to perpetual servitude" (Stow 1977: 294). This is backed up by the apostle Paul, who compares Christians to a free woman and Jews to a slave woman (Gal 4:21–31). The harsh treatment of Jews is justified because it shows in practice what is true in principle. It is hoped that this performative enactment of the Jews' servile status will persuade them of the truth of Christianity so that, desiring to be set free, they will become Christian. Berger summarizes the argument thus: "Because Jews are tolerated for two purposes both of which serve Christian aims (to testify to Christian truth and to make possible the Jews' conversion), it is therefore appropriate that they be subordinated to Christians" (Berger 1979: 45). The problem, for Paul IV, is that Jews are becoming prosperous, living in nice houses alongside Christians, and even taking Christian servants to work for them. This undermines the message of the Gospel and is a violation of the true nature of things because it makes Jews look like superiors of Christians or at least equals. Therefore, Jews should be stripped of their privileges and confined to poor ghettos to remind them of their true place in the world, in the hope that they will see their miserable condition for what it is and convert to Christianity.

Fourteen years later, Pope Pius V began *Hebraeorum Gens* in the same way: the Jews live wretched lives hated by all, which is their punishment for having murdered Christ. Up until now, Christian piety has allowed them to live here for two reasons: so that seeing them might remind Christians of Jesus' death and so that they might convert to Christianity. However, they have become so harmful and dangerous to society that we can no longer tolerate them. They practice magic; they draw respectable women into prostitution; they are accomplices of thieves; and their usury has drained Christian nations of their wealth. We are forced, therefore, to expel them. Any Jew found outside the two remaining ghettos in two months' time will be subjected to slavery (Anon 1727: 296–8).

Some scholars point out that the Pope was not acting as the head of the Church but in his secular role as the sovereign of the Papal States (Mattei 2021). It is doubtful how relevant such a distinction is since obviously it does not change what he did or his reasons for doing so. Perhaps the only difference it makes is to show that the Pope's action should not be taken as official Church policy.

A more pertinent point is that in acting thus, Pius V was radically breaking with Catholic tradition and even with the legal opinion of the day, which judged expulsion to be legally invalid (Stow 2015: 381, 383). Doubtless, he had been influenced by the (by then) centuries of national expulsions of Jews. The Pope's actions were more in line with contemporary political practice than with the traditional wisdom of the Catholic Church, which had always forbidden hostility against Jews. Nonetheless, the early modern concern with national and religious purity led to theological arguments in favor of expulsion, even coming from the Pope himself. Some of these arguments have since been nullified by the Second Vatican Council, which in 1964 definitively declared that "not all Jews at the time of Jesus, nor Jews as a class since that time, including contemporary Jews, can be held collectively guilty for killing Jesus Christ" (D'Costa 2014: 122). This served to refute the common medieval idea that the Jews were guilty of killing Jesus and therefore deserved inferior treatment. But this idea held sway for hundreds of years and served to buttress some of the most severe anti-immigration policies in European history.

Catholic Immigration Policy Today

Pope Pius V's expulsion of the Jews was the closest thing to an official Church position on immigration in medieval Europe, yet, as we saw, it is not accurately understood as such. It is another instance of confusion between national identity and religious identity, in which the Pope, the *religious* leader of all of Europe, invokes *religious* principles in his capacity as *state* sovereign to eject the religious "other" from the *state*. At that time, there was no official Church teaching on migration. But since the nineteenth century, the Catholic magisterium has published far more on migration than any other Christian group. The content of these theological writings gives a strikingly different impression from what we saw in the medieval and early modern eras.

The Catholic Church's contemporary teaching on immigration can be summarized as a call to "welcome, protect, promote and integrate" immigrants regardless of their nationality or religious affiliation (*Fratelli Tutti,* para. 129), yet in a way that does not abolish the "right of every country to pursue an immigration policy that promotes the common good" (*Erga migrantes caritas Christi*, para. 29). The rights of the immigrant and the rights of the nation-state are held in tension, with priority given to the rights of the disadvantaged immigrant. Pope John Paul II, after affirming the right to migrate, adds that "the exercise of such a right is to be regulated, because practicing it indiscriminately may do harm and be detrimental to the common good of the community that receives the migrant" (John Paul II 2001). The Catholic Church thus permits states to control their borders but not absolutely. State sovereignty is subordinate to the needs of the migrant and the responsibility of rich and powerful nations to support those fleeing oppressive and war-torn situations.

In the nineteenth century, Vatican directives concerning migration were localized, offering guidance to clergy in specific situations (Baggio 2010). But the vast numbers of refugees following World War II led (as it did for the UN) to a more generalized response. In 1951, Pope Pius XII issued *Exsul Familia Nazarethana* (The Exile of the Family of Nazareth), which takes its title from the forced migration of Jesus, Mary, and Joseph to Egypt (cf. Matt 2:13–15). This apostolic constitution begins by recognizing the sufferings and hardships that come with migration, and holds up the Holy Family as the "model and protector" of every migrant. It then catalogs the ways the Church has shown compassion to migrants throughout history, followed by a set of instructions to clergy on the pastoral and spiritual care of migrants.

The Vatican did not only give statements, however. That same year, the Pope established a new Vatican department, the "Superior Council for Emigrants," which in 1988 was renamed the "Pontifical Council for the Pastoral Care of Migrants and Refugees" and then in 2017 became the "Migrants and Refugees section" in the Dicastery for Integral Human Development. Its purpose is to offer centralized and coordinated support to Catholics around the world engaging in the welcome and accompaniment of migrants and refugees.

The next significant step came in 1969 with the release of *De Pastorali Migratorum Cura* (On the Pastoral Care of Migrants), which for the first time used the language of "migrant rights." According to this papal instruction, everyone has the right to a homeland, the right to emigrate and immigrate, the right to preserve the unity of the family, and the right to keep one's native language and culture. All Catholics, priests and laity, are responsible for the protection of migrants, and dialog with governments is necessary to ensure that migrants' rights are upheld (Nanko-Fernández 2015: 6–9).

In 1992, two Pontifical Councils including the (then-named) Pontifical Council for the Pastoral Care of Migrants jointly published "Refugees: A Challenge to Solidarity." This text begins by quoting Pope John Paul II, who called the growing number of refugees in the world "perhaps the greatest tragedy of all the human tragedies of our time." After defining various types of refugees and refugee situations, it reaffirms the aforementioned rights and along with them affirms the right to seek asylum given in the UN's 1948 Universal Declaration of Human Rights. It then addresses the "responsibilities of states," which include the following injunction:

> Democratic and economically developed States cannot remain indifferent in the face of such a tragic situation. Inaction or a meagre commitment on the part of these States would blatantly contradict the principles that they rightly consider the basis of their culture, established on the equal dignity of every human person.

What is significant about this statement is that it explicitly calls not just for welcome and support at the private individual level but for immigration policies at the state level that do the same.

In 2004, the Pontifical Council for the Pastoral Care of Migrants and Itinerant People published *Erga migrantes caritas Christi* (The Love of Christ Towards Migrants). This text goes deeper into the underlying causes of migration and explores the basic international structures that make migration necessary. It calls for states to "guarantee the rights of all migrants" and instructs everyone "to reject all sentiments and manifestations of xenophobia and racism on the part of host communities" (para. 30).

In 2020, Pope Francis issued the encyclical *Fratelli Tutti* (All Brothers), a strong affirmation of the brother- and sisterhood of all humanity that condemns nationalism and the protection of self-interest. The pope calls for solidarity with all human beings regardless of nationality or culture and speaks against "those who organize themselves in a way that prevents any foreign presence that might threaten their identity and their closed and self-referential structures" (para. 102). It is not a naïve document. The pope shows a keen awareness that anti-immigration sentiment can be religiously motivated. He writes, "There are those who appear to feel encouraged or at least permitted by their faith to support varieties of narrow and violent nationalism, xenophobia and contempt, and even the mistreatment of those who are different" (para. 86). In an era of increasing nationalism, much of which does not distinguish between religious affiliation and national identity, the pope comes down strongly in favor of immigrant welcome as the only authentically Catholic response for everyone who sees their faith not only as a communal identity but also as a commitment to a way of life and treatment of others.

As we have seen, Pope Francis' strong pro-immigration stance is not remotely innovative or a break from Catholic tradition but stands in continuity with it. Yet, despite this strong injunction to welcome strangers from the Vatican, many Catholics remain wary of immigrants. As we saw in the above section, anti-immigration policy is paradoxically more likely in countries with a strong Catholic majority. Roy (2018) writes that "in Catholic countries the populist electorate . . . do not at all follow the call from the Church to be more lenient towards migrants." This paradox is explained by the distinction between ways of viewing religion. In majority Catholic countries, their faith is seen more as a part of national identity that they wish to preserve, whereas in countries where Catholicism is a minority, the Vatican's stance is taken more seriously as indicative of faithful Catholicism.

A Brief Note on the Orthodox Church

Space does not permit a comparable treatment of Eastern Christianity to that of the West. In the wake of the forced migrations from Afghanistan, Syria, and Ukraine, among others, immigration is an increasingly contested topic among Eastern Christians. Yet the Orthodox Church has almost no official teaching on immigration. This striking absence, especially in contrast to Catholicism, is not anomalous but a common feature of the tradition. As one scholar writes:

> The Orthodox theological tradition has no specific "Theology of Migration". . . . The Orthodox churches in general are not in the habit of making public statements in immediate response to ethical or socio-political issues that emerge from time to time. Individual leaders, teachers, and theologians of the church may speak or write and make their opinions public. These theological opinions carry some weight, depending on the personalities that make them, but they tend not to be binding on the church. They can serve as guidelines for the faithful to exercise their freedom and discretion in ethical, social, and political domains.
>
> *(George 2014: 63–4)*

Similarly, Leuştean writes (2019: 9) that "the Eastern Orthodox world stands out due to the lack of a systematic and widely agreed approach on how to engage with the concept of the 'other' and, thus, with migrants." This, he says, makes Orthodox Christianity vulnerable to political manipulation. The growing number of migrants in the world, forced and otherwise,

> has been both a crisis and an opportunity for Orthodox churches. It has been a crisis due to the lack of a theological reflection on humanitarian issues and social engagement with forced migration. As a result, some Orthodox clergy incited the masses in support of right-wing nationalism and populism dehumanizing the displaced populations. It has also been an opportunity as some clergy began to question the validity of

nationalist discourses from some of their top hierarchy and offered their own unsanctioned support to migrants.

(Leuștean 2019: 9)

A partial exception to this silence comes from the "Holy and Great Synod of the Orthodox Church" held in 2016. Patterned along the lines of the ancient Ecumenical Councils, its intention was to make a series of pronouncements that would be binding on all Orthodox Christians. One of the documents issued from the council addressed the issue of migrants and refugees:

We appeal therefore first of all to those able to remove the causes for the creation of the refugee crisis to take the necessary positive decisions. We call on the civil authorities, the Orthodox faithful and the other citizens of the countries in which they have sought refuge and continue to seek refuge to accord them every possible assistance, even from out of their own insufficiency.

(Holy and Great Council 2016)

However, four of the 14 self-governing churches (including the largest, the Russian Orthodox Church) refused to attend the synod or to accept it as representing a pan-Orthodox consensus. Consequently, the synod's pronouncements have not succeeded in acquiring the status of an authoritative Orthodox statement.

The lack of top-level guidance on immigration policy has led to a great diversity of positions on immigration among Orthodox religious leaders. Yet, as we have seen, the vast quantity of guidance from the Catholic Church has not led to any less diversity of Catholic positions. However, in the Catholic case, it is clearer who is in line with the teachings of their Church and who is not.

American Evangelicals and the Bible

Setting the Scene: Demographic Trends

More than any other religious demographic in the United States, Evangelical attitudes to immigration are in the public eye. This is partly because they represent such a large proportion of the

American public (in 2015, the Pew Research Center estimated that 25% of US adults self-identified as Evangelical – see Wormald 2015) and partly because white Evangelicals stand out as the religious group most opposed to immigration (McDaniel et al. 2011: 222). Melkonian-Hoover and Kellstedt write that

> although other religious interest groups, including mainline Protestant, Jewish, and Catholic organizations have been active in supporting immigration reform for some time, they are less visible in the media these days, as their support for such issues is often taken as a given.
>
> *(2019: 51)*

There is no "official" Evangelical position on immigration policy. Evangelicalism is not a denomination but a "flavor" of Christianity that began in the eighteenth century, defined by particular theological emphases, style of worship, and commonly shared resources, books, conferences, public speakers, symbols, and vocabulary. Over 400 million people in the world are classified as Evangelical, most of whom reside in the Global South. The United States is the only Western nation with a sufficiently large population of Evangelicals to be politically noteworthy (Zurlo et al. 2022: 76). Yet, in the last two decades, a gap has been growing between white American Evangelicals and all other kinds (black or Hispanic Evangelicals in the United States and Evangelicals everywhere else in the world – Melkonian-Hoover & Kellstedt 2019: 8). White Evangelicals' alliance with the US Republican Party has led to their placing a stronger emphasis on aspects of their faith that align with right-wing politics and a growing suspicion of anyone who claims that Christianity also supports left-wing positions, such as a more pro-immigration stance. Yet this opposition to immigration is a recent phenomenon in both Evangelicalism and the Republican Party. Immigration has only become one of the dividing lines between the two political parties in the last decade (Cremer 2023: 200). Likewise, Evangelicals were also more favorable toward immigration in preceding decades (Melkonian-Hoover & Kellstedt 2019: 28–36).

Another recent phenomenon has been the rise of a new demographic: the nonpracticing Evangelical. Since its inception, Evangelicals had defined themselves precisely as the "real" (i.e., practicing) Christians in protest against nominal or superficial forms of Christianity (Walls 1996: 82–3). In the United States, this self-identification no longer applies. People have started to self-identify as Evangelical even if they neither believe in Evangelical tenets of faith nor regularly attend church (Burge 2020). Yet, where nonpracticing members of other denominations tend to be more politically liberal, here the opposite is the case. Cremer writes that

> America's nonpracticing cultural Evangelicals have proven not just more politically conservative but also significantly more sympathetic towards right-wing populist positions and candidates than their churchgoing brethren. During the 2016 primaries political scientist Geoffrey Layman observed, for instance, that "Trump does best among Evangelicals with one key trait: they don't really go to Church."
>
> *(2023: 231)*

As we saw in Europe in the previous section, social science studies have shown that anti-immigration sentiment is stronger among nonpracticing Evangelicals than among those who attend church regularly (McDaniel et al. 2011: 221; Melkonian-Hoover & Kellstedt 2019: 8, 139; Stroope et al. 2021: 8). Mark Galli, at the time editor in chief of *Christianity Today* magazine, told Cremer that "Evangelicals who don't go to church are very anti-immigration, whereas those who do go to church are much more open to it" (cited in Cremer 2023: 232). The warmer stance toward immigrants among practicing Evangelicals is most likely because they encounter a more welcoming attitude in the substance of Christianity, whether through sermons, popular books, or Bible studies. This further suggests that the theologically and biblically literate are more likely to be pro-immigration.

The tendency of Evangelical elites to support immigration, however, is less influential than might be expected. One of Evangelicalism's defining features is a populist approach to faith

(Stackhouse 2022: 35). While they respect the opinion of biblical scholars, Evangelicals believe that the message of the Bible is accessible to anyone regardless of education level. That explains why politicians with no theological training can gain support from Evangelical voters by citing Bible verses out of context. It also means that laypeople are less likely to listen to what the "establishment elites" have to say about immigration. This suspicion of institutional authority accounts for what Melkonian-Hoover and Kellstedt call a "fault line between white evangelical elites (i.e., denominational, church, and parachurch leaders) and the white evangelical laity, with the former increasing supportive of [immigration] and the latter favoring more strictly conservative approaches" (2019: 8).

Although all Christians draw on the Bible as a resource, the lack of ecclesial authority in Evangelicalism combined with the populist approach has placed the Bible front and center of debates far more visibly than in other Christian groups. That is why an exploration of what the Bible has to say on immigration, while an essential part of any Christian view, fits most naturally with the Evangelical conversation. We now turn to explore the Bible's message on immigration policy as it appears in contemporary debates within Evangelicalism.

Immigration in the Bible

The theme of migration is so pervasive in the Bible that one scholar called the Bible "a literary tapestry woven from the stories of migrants" (Hoppe 2007: 209). Most of the Bible's major events involve migration. The people of Israel flee slavery in Egypt; later on, they are exiled from their own land to Babylon. In the New Testament, Jesus' family flees to Egypt, and persecution scatters the early Christians throughout the Roman Empire. Additionally, almost all the major characters of the Bible migrate: Adam and Eve, Abraham, Jacob, Joseph, Moses, David, Elijah, Jeremiah, Ruth, Daniel, and Esther – to name a few.

However, not all biblical references to migration are universally recognized as relevant to immigration. The key problem confronting any Christian who seeks an immigration policy in the Bible is the question of how to apply a complex text written in another age and culture to the concerns of the present day. Not all usages of the Bible in debates over immigration policy have the sophistication and nuance that come with scholarly expertise. Nor do they all have a sober grasp of how challenging it can be to interpret an ancient text in which many contemporary notions ("nation-state," "border," "government," "law," "human rights," indeed even words like "justice," "stranger," and "welcome") are either completely absent or carry a strikingly different sense. To invoke a scriptural passage without regard for its historical context is to risk misinterpreting it. Yet to take this context into account may make it harder to see the text's contemporary relevance. These difficulties are so familiar to scholars that many have abandoned the possibility of any contemporary relevance to the Bible. Yet giving up is not an option for any community for which scripture is God's revelation of how people should live, among other things. The task must be attempted.

Nevertheless, to claim exegetical support for a position by no means proves its validity. Bible scholars do not all agree. Almost every position on immigration can claim the support of at least one expert. Academic credentials are no safeguard against political bias. University professors are no more immune than anyone else to being swept along by faddish ideas and carried along in the current of the prevailing ideology. A cursory knowledge of scholarship in previous centuries, with some of its colonialist and misogynistic presuppositions, makes this evident. It would be either arrogant or naïve to suppose that academics today are free of the cultural blinkers that we see so clearly in our predecessors.

The problem of applying the Bible's message is particularly acute when it comes to the question of whether a moral precept is only for private individuals or for national policy. The Hebrew Bible did not distinguish between religion and politics: the nation of Israel and the Israelite religion were one and the same. By contrast, Christianity began within Judaism as a movement that dissociated itself from any particular nationality. While nations throughout history have self-identified as Christian, Christianity has never been associated exclusively with a single nation. Jesus also inaugurated a new covenant with a new set of moral and behavioral instructions. This did not render the Hebrew Bible obsolete: it still reveals God's character and moral principles for human behavior. But the laws in the *Torah* are not *ipso facto* binding on Christians. Nor is the New Testament unambiguous in its political application, having been written during a period when Christians had little political power and were not yet faced with the question of how to govern. This makes it possible to interpret Jesus' moral mandates in multiple ways. For example, some regard his command to turn the other cheek (Matthew 5:39) as a matter of personal morality; for others, it entails pacifism at the national level.

Consequently, there is a broad range of views on how Christian ethics relates to politics. One extreme is the traditional Anabaptist view that Christians should have nothing to do with politics. The other extreme is known as Christian nationalism, holding that Christians should use the government to implement Christian values at the political and legal levels (Wolfe 2022). This view does not imply a radical identification of church and state. It can take the form of pluralistic governance that permits freedom of religion, but it would do so only if freedom of religion is seen as a Christian value by the government.

Between these two extremes, but closer to the Anabaptist position, is a view common among many Americans, which we might call Christian libertarianism. Originally articulated by John Locke, one of the principal sources of inspiration behind the US Constitution holds that the government's role is not to enact Christian values but to protect property rights. For example, Edwards (2018: 262) writes that "mercy and compassion are demanded of individuals, not public policy for the state" (p. 262). Similarly, Moreland writes, "the state is not to be in the business of showing compassion. . . . That is an individual moral responsibility" (2013: 7). Most starkly, Strand (2015) writes,

> the church should be on the frontlines taking care of refugees and displaced peoples, but its [*sic*] not clear the American government faces a similar obligation to admit refugees because the American government is not a charity organization or the church and we should be glad that it is not.

No answer to these questions has commanded universal support among Christians. They must be borne in mind as we survey the ways the Bible is used in contemporary immigration debates.

Who Is the Stranger?

The following quotations are adapted from the NRSV (New Revised Standard Version):

> When a *ger* resides with you in your land, you shall not oppress the *ger*. The *ger* who resides with you shall be to you as the citizen among you; you shall love the *ger* as yourself, for you were *gerim* [the plural of *ger*] in the land of Egypt.
> *(Leviticus 19:33–34)*

> There shall be for both you and the *ger* a single statute, a perpetual statute throughout your generations; you and the *ger* shall be alike before the Lord. You and the *ger* who resides with you shall have the same law and the same ordinance.
> *(Numbers 15:15–16)*

> You shall love the *ger*, for you were *gerim* in the land of Egypt.
> *(Deuteronomy 10:19)*

These verses contain two foundational principles repeated throughout the *Torah*: (1) equality before the law of citizen and *ger* and (2) love and welcome for the *ger*.

English translations render *ger* variously as "stranger," "sojourner," "foreigner," "alien," or "resident alien." But not all foreigners are in view here. A wealthy merchant, an independent traveler, or a soldier in an attacking army does not count as *ger*. The Hebrew Bible has four words for foreigner:

1. *Nokri* or *nekhar* denotes any foreigner, usually one living in a foreign land or passing through Israel. They are independent and neither need nor seek financial support or integration into Israel.

2. *Zar* can be used interchangeably with *nokri* but is sometimes used for an Israelite who is excluded from a particular activity (e.g., a non-Levite in a cultic rite). It could loosely be translated as "whoever does not belong to the group being discussed."
3. *Toshav* is usually a passing traveler or hired slave whose presence is usually temporary.
4. *Ger* (plural *gerim*) is the most significant word. The Torah or Pentateuch contains over 70 laws about the *ger*, 30 of which command legal equality with citizens.

The definition of *ger* has been hotly disputed in the context of American debates over "illegal" or "undocumented" immigration. Hoffmeier (2009: 52) argues that the *ger* is a lawful foreign resident, that is, someone who has "followed legal procedures to obtain recognized standing as a resident alien." The biblical passages about the *ger* apply only to those to whom the government permits entry. If the government has not officially given them entrance, then they are not *ger*, so the Bible does not require anyone to love and welcome them. Hoffmeier's position gives the government absolute power to decide whom to give and whom to refuse the status of *ger* and leaves the Bible without any instructions for the government to help with immigration policy.

While Hoffmeier's definition has not been accepted in scholarship, it has been influential in US politics. His work formed the basis of a Bible study in the White House during the Trump presidency (Drollinger 2019). The study was attended by members of the US Congress and the White House cabinet, providing a Christian justification for the government to expel undocumented immigrants.

But according to most other scholars (Carroll R. 2013; Glanville 2018; Koehler et al. 2000; Wielenga 2020; Wright 2004; Zehnder 2021), the *ger* is not a "legal immigrant" but a displaced foreigner who lacks access to basic resources because they do not have the two sources of financial stability in the ancient world: family connections and land; they are probably unable to return home. In this case, it is not down to the government whether someone is classified as *ger*; this is determined by their situation of social and financial disadvantage and instability, and it is the government's duty to offer them protection and provision.

Are National Territories and Borders Divinely Ordained?

> When the Most High apportioned the nations, when he divided humankind, he fixed the boundaries of the peoples according to the number of the gods.
>
> (Deuteronomy 32:8)

> From one ancestor [God] made all nations to inhabit the whole earth, and he allotted the times of their existence and the boundaries of the places where they would live.
>
> (Acts 17:26)

From these verses, it is argued (Drollinger 2019; Edwards 2018; Zehnder 2021) that (1) national borders and boundaries are God's design; (2) the current territories and borders of each nation are God-given; and (3) cosmopolitanism, open borders, and free movement of peoples are excluded as valid Christian positions. God is not in favor of a borderless world.

Critics of this argument object that it gives divine approval to whatever national territories and borders happen to exist right now, regardless of their history or of what violent conquest may have been used to determine them. In practice, this means

> justifying the results of a historical process of carving up the world's territory between states that primarily has been achieved through the force of arms. . . . [This view] cannot help but recognize as valid a nation's right to its de facto territorial holdings – however it has come by them – at least if it has controlled those holdings long enough for the world to get used to it.
>
> *(Gibney 2004: 39)*

According to these critics, the above Bible passages should not be seen as a divine endorsement of permanent boundaries because Israel's boundaries shifted several times even within biblical history (2 Samuel 5:1–5; 1 Kings 4:21; 12:16; 2 Kings 18:13). Furthermore, God forbids violent conquest to extend borders (Zehnder 2021: 61). Rather, the above verses underscore divine sovereignty over history, a common theme throughout the Bible (Glanville & Glanville 2021). The Christian tradition later developed a distinction between God's "permissive will" in evil actions that God does not prevent and God's "active will" in things God directly does. Violent conquest would fall under the former category but not the latter.

Some scholars argue further that biblically, possession of land does not entail absolute control over borders (Heimburger 2018; Katanacho 2005; Wright 2004). God owns everything (Psalm 50:12; 24:1), so human "ownership" is in fact stewardship. This is evidenced by Leviticus 25:23 in which God says to Israel, "The land shall not be sold in perpetuity, for the land is mine. With me you are but aliens [*gerim*] and tenants [*toshavim*]." This verse strikingly gives the status of immigrants even to national citizens. Their right to the land is revocable should they behave in a way contrary to the law of God, who is the land's true owner. Heimburger writes that

> God delegates governmental authority, and so government cannot be understood as sovereign in an ultimate sense. . . . Authority over immigration is not plenary or unlimited. [Therefore] Authority over territory is divinely granted, but this authority and the authority over immigration is checked by the requirements of the one Sovereign [i.e. God].
> *(Heimburger 2018: 113–14, 124)*

God's ultimate possession of the land still applies to land that God "gives" to people. The language of "gift," according to Wright, is

> not just an arbitrary and unconditional gift, but a constituent grant that formed part of the total package of their relationship henceforth. Israel's enjoyment of the covenanted *gift*, therefore, demanded their reciprocal obligations to the covenanting *giver*. . . . Israel could not treat the gift of the land as

> a license to abuse it, because *the land was still YHWH's land.* He retained the ultimate title of ownership and therefore also the ultimate right of moral authority over how it was used.
>
> *(Wright 2004: 93; see also Orlinsky 1986)*

This understanding of the biblical picture of national territory has radical implications for immigration policy. Without promoting open borders, it strips national citizens of any sovereign right to refuse entry to whomever they please. Rather, they must discern God's will for immigration policy.

Are Governments Divinely Ordained?

> Jesus said to [the pharisees], "Give to the emperor the things that are the emperor's, and to God the things that are God's."
>
> (Mark 12:17)

> Jesus answered [Pilate], "You would have no power over me unless it had been given you from above."
>
> (John 19:11)

> Let every person be subject to the governing authorities; for there is no authority except from God, and those authorities that exist have been instituted by God. Therefore whoever resists authority resists what God has appointed, and those who resist will incur judgement. For rulers are not a terror to good conduct, but to bad. Do you wish to have no fear of the authority? Then do what is good, and you will receive its approval; for it is God's servant for your good. But if you do what is wrong, you should be afraid, for the authority does not bear the sword in vain! It is the servant of God to execute wrath on the wrongdoer.
>
> (Romans 13:1)

Based on these passages, it is argued (Drollinger 2019; Edwards 2018; Hoffmeier 2009; Sessions 2018; Swain 2011) that (1) a government is justified in whatever immigration policy it adopts because whatever policy it adopts is authorized by God and (2) a government's primary responsibility is to protect its citizens. This means that, in Drollinger's words, "for a government to be pleasing to God and receive His blessing, it has no option but to protect its citizenry from illegal immigration" (Drollinger 2019).

Critics of this argument object (Soerens & Yang 2009: 95; Glanville & Glanville 2021; Butner Jr. 2023b) that Romans 13 is not absolute: it instructs Christians to be lawful citizens except where this conflicts with their higher allegiance to God. Christians have interpreted Romans 13 this way throughout history when finding themselves under unjust governments, such as the Nazi regime or apartheid. In fact, the Bible is full of examples of civil disobedience, such as when the apostle Peter said, "we must obey God rather than any human authority" (Acts 5:29). Indeed, this interpretation of Romans 13 could be regarded logically as the only possible one. If someone obeys civil authorities because scripture says so, this implies scripture's higher authority, meaning anyone who commands disobedience to scripture must be disobeyed.

In fact, Romans 13 gives no guidance at all on what kind of immigration policy a nation should adopt. It is usually invoked for two reasons: (1) to denounce support for undocumented (illegal) immigrants and (2) to justify passivity regarding a nation's immigration law. But as Hadas (2020: 238) notes, the passage "can reasonably be interpreted as condemning illegal immigration but not as condoning making immigration illegal in the first place." In other words, it says nothing at all about whether a government is justified in giving, refusing, or revoking legal statuses to immigrants.

Does Jesus Identify With All Immigrants?

> Then the king [i.e. Jesus] will say to those at his right hand, "Come, you that are blessed by my Father, inherit the kingdom prepared for you from the foundation of the world; for I was hungry and you gave me food, I was thirsty and you gave me something to drink, I was a stranger and you welcomed me, I was naked and you gave me clothing, I was sick and you took care of me, I was in prison and you visited me." Then the righteous will answer him, "Lord, when was it that we saw you hungry and gave you food, or thirsty and gave you something to drink? And when was it that we saw you a stranger and welcomed you, or naked and gave you clothing? And when was it that we saw you sick or in prison and visited you?" And the king will answer them,

> "Truly I tell you, just as you did it to one of the least of these who are members of my family, you did it to me."
>
> (Matthew 25:34–40)

From this passage (and the succeeding one, Matthew 25:41–46, in which those who did not do the same things are sent to eternal punishment), it is argued that a Christian's eternal destiny is dependent on their behavior toward those in need, including "the stranger." Jesus identifies himself with the stranger (Greek *xenos* – a much broader term than the Hebrew *ger*), so if we welcome strangers, it is as if we were welcoming Jesus himself, and if we turn away strangers, it is as if we were turning away Jesus himself.

Critics of this argument object (Hoffmeier 2009: 148) that Jesus does not identify himself with any stranger but only with those who are "members of his family," namely, Christians or perhaps only the disciples to whom he was speaking. In response, defenders suggest (Butner Jr. 2023a; Glanville & Glanville 2021) that "members of Jesus' family" is understood more broadly elsewhere in the New Testament (e.g., in Matthew 5:22; Mark 9:27). However, even if this rejoinder is successful, it does not establish whether this passage should be understood as applying to national legislation or only to private individual welcome of strangers.

Was Jesus Himself a Refugee?

> An angel of the Lord appeared to Joseph in a dream and said, "Get up, take the child and his mother, and flee to Egypt, and remain there until I tell you; for Herod is about to search for the child, to destroy him." Then Joseph got up, took the child and his mother by night, and went to Egypt, and remained there until the death of Herod.
>
> (Matthew 2:13–14)

This is the most frequently quoted Bible passage in Christian discussions about immigration because it recounts the time Jesus himself fled to Egypt with his family to save his life. However, the significance of this passage is rarely spelled out. Proponents of immigrant welcome (Cornell 2014) speak about Jesus' identification with refugees. Those more opposed to immigration aver that, despite this personal experience, it is striking that Jesus said nothing in later life about the treatment of refugees (Hoffmeier 2009: 135). This latter claim might be refuted by recalling Matthew 25 above.

Two treatments of this passage go deeper. Butner (2023a) engages in a thought experiment, imagining how Jesus and his family might have fared as refugees in today's world. His purpose is to highlight the severe challenges and hardships they would have undergone, with a view to altering Christian attitudes toward contemporary refugees. Aspray (2024) suggests that, through identification with Jesus, Christians ought to identify with refugees such that they are no longer seen as "other." However, both of these treatments are unclear as to how far these insights are meant to affect not only private individual behavior but also immigration policy.

Conclusion

Few can deny the Bible's strong and pervasive call to welcome immigrants and to give them the same legal privileges as citizens. Granted, this welcome neither necessarily implies an open border policy nor is it indiscriminate: it places the emphasis on displaced immigrants who lack access to basic resources and security. Evangelicals opposed to immigration do not tend to find explicit anti-immigrant content in the Bible. For them, the anti-immigration position depends on limiting the Bible's welcoming mandate to the private moral sphere or to unique historical circumstances that no longer apply today, stripping them of any contemporary political relevance. Rather, the anti-immigration position looks to biblical texts that give warrant to a government to do whatever it pleases and to prioritize the well-being of citizens over strangers.

Yet any reading of the Bible that insists on its political applicability is a double-edged sword. If the Christian thing to do is to welcome immigrants, but the nation does not want to welcome immigrants, should Christians use political power to override the national will and welcome immigrants anyway? To answer "yes" would set a precedent for Christian use of political power that may be deployed in other areas. The pro-immigration stance depends on a conceived relationship between church and state that has proven itself dangerous in the past, leading to histories of oppression, violence, and abuse.

One example of such oppressive use of political power is the cozy relationship between church and state that medieval and early modern Catholicism enjoyed, leading to the expulsion of those who did not share the faith of the nation. The political and religious leaders sought to align religious identity with national identity, purifying the nation of unbelievers by ejecting any who refused to convert. Instead of recognizing Jews as "the stranger" whom the Bible enjoins us to protect and welcome, they turned them into displaced strangers who were forced to seek protection and welcome elsewhere.

The gradual loss of power that the Church experienced between the sixteenth and twentieth centuries may have made it less capable of implementing its religious principles in national politics, but it also served to clarify what those religious principles really were. The overwhelmingly strong call to welcome the stranger issued from the Vatican since the twentieth century is in perfect accord with the message of the Bible, with the difference that the Vatican, as a living present-day voice, is able to speak without ambiguity into the contemporary situation. What the Catholic Church teaches is now abundantly clear to anyone for whom "Catholic" is not merely a cultural or national identity marker but a lived faith commitment to a set of practices. Welcoming strangers is a practice not only for individuals but also for nations.

References

Al Jazeera. (2019). "Why Will Poland Not Take in Any Muslims?" November 8. Viewed from: www.aljazeera.com/program/upfront/2019/11/8/why-will-poland-not-take-in-any-muslims [Date accessed: 13 September 2024].

Anon. (1727). *Magnum Bullarium Romanum*. Vol. 2. Luxemburgi: Sumptibus Andreae Chevalier.

Aquinas, St. Thomas. (1911). *Summa Theologiae*. New York: Benziger Bros.

Aspray, Barnabas. (2024). "Jesus Was a Refugee: Unpacking the Theological Implications". *Modern Theology* 40(2).

Augustine of Hippo. (1887). *On Christian Doctrine*. Vol. 2. Edited by P. Schaff. Christian Literature Company.

Baggio, Fabio. (2010). "The Migrant Ministry: A Constant Concern of the Catholic Church". *Asian Christian Review* 4(2):47–69.

Bell, David Andreas, and Zan Strabac. (2020). "Exclusion of Muslims in Eastern Europe and Western Europe: A Comparative Analysis of Anti-Muslim Attitudes in France, Norway, Poland and Czech Republic". *International Journal on Minority and Group Rights* 28(1):117–42.

Berger, David. (1979). "Cum Nimis Absurdum and the Conversion of the Jews". *The Jewish Quarterly Review* 70(1):41–9.

Biggar, Nigel, Richard Ekins, and John Finnis. (2022). *From the Channel to Rwanda: Three Essays on the Morality of Asylum*. London: Policy Exchange.

Burge, Ryan. (2020). "So, Why Is Evangelicalism Not Declining? Because Non-Attenders Are Taking on the Label". *Religion in Public*. Viewed from: https://religioninpublic.blog/2020/12/10/-why-is-evangelicalism-not-declining-because-non-attenders-are-taking-on-the-label/ [Date accessed: 16 October 2024].

Butner Jr., D. Glenn. (2023a). *Jesus the Refugee: Ancient Injustice and Modern Solidarity*. Fortress Press.

Butner Jr., D. Glenn. (2023b). "Undocumented Prudent Immigrants: De-Centering Romans 13 and Rule of Law in Immigration Ethics". *Studies in Christian Ethics* 36(1):62–83.

Carroll, R., M. Daniel. (2013). "Welcoming the Stranger: Toward a Theology of Immigration in Deuteronomy". in *For Our Good Always: Studies on the Message and Influence of Deuteronomy in Honor of Daniel I: Block*, edited by J. S. DeRouchie, J. Gile, and K. J. Turner. Winona Lake, IN: Eisenbrauns.

Chazan, Robert. (2023). "Medieval Antisemitism". Pp. 20–7 in *The Routledge History of Antisemitism*, edited by M. Weitzman, R. J. Williams, and J. Wald. Taylor & Francis.

Church in Wales. (n.d.). "Bishops Urge Government to Withdraw Rwanda Bill". *Church in Wales*. Viewed from: www.churchinwales.org.uk/en/news-and-events/bishops-urge-government-to-withdraw-rwanda-bill/ [Date accessed: 1 April 2024].

Church of England. (n.d.). "Migration". *The Church of England*. Viewed from: www.churchofengland.org/about/social-transformation/migration [Date accessed: 1 April 2024].

Coppen, Luke. (2023). "How Steep Is Poland's Drop in Mass Attendance?" January 18. Viewed from: www.pillarcatholic.

com/p/how-steep-is-polands-drop-in-mass-attendance [Date accessed: 23 October 2024].

Cornell, Deirdre. (2014). *Jesus Was a Migrant*. Maryknoll: Orbis Books.

Cremer, Tobias. (2023). *The Godless Crusade*. Cambridge: Cambridge University Press.

D'Costa, Gavin. (2014). *Vatican II: Catholic Doctrines on Jews and Muslims*. Oxford: Oxford University Press.

de Boer, Martinus C. (2011). *Galatians: A Commentary*. La Vergne, US: Westminster John Knox Press.

Drollinger, Ralph. (2019). "What the Bible Says about Our Illegal Immigration Problem". *Capitol Ministries*. Viewed from: https://capmin.org/bible-says-illegal-immigration-problem/ [Date accessed: 20 February 2024].

Edwards, James R. (2018). "Biblical Prudence and American Immigration". Pp. 261–85 in *Debating Immigration*, edited by C. M. Swain. Cambridge: University Press.

Escarcena, Juan Pablo Aris. (2020). "Christian Charity as the Last Line of Defense for Migrants in Ventimiglia". in *Europe and the Refugee Response: A Crisis of Values?, Routledge Studies in Development, Displacement and Resettlement*, edited by E. M. Goździak, I. Main, and B. Suter. New York: Routledge.

George, Kondothra M. (2014). "Theology of Migration in the Orthodox Tradition". Pp. 63–76 in *Theology of Migration in the Abrahamic Religions*, edited by E. Padilla and P. C. Phan. New York: Palgrave Macmillan.

Gerber, Jane S. (1992). *The Jews of Spain: A History of the Sephardic Experience*. The Free Press.

Gerber, Jane S. (2012). "Turning Point". Pp. 224–43 in *The Wiley-Blackwell History of Jews and Judaism*. John Wiley & Sons, Ltd.

Gibney, Matthew J. (2004). *The Ethics and Politics of Asylum: Liberal Democracy and the Response to Refugees*. Cambridge: Cambridge University Press.

Glanville, Mark. (2018). *Adopting the Stranger as Kindred in Deuteronomy*. Atlanta: Society of Biblical Literature.

Glanville, Mark, and Luke Glanville. (2021). *Refuge Reimagined: Biblical Kinship in Global Politics*. Downers Grove: InterVarsity Press.

Górak-Sosnowska, Katarzyna, and Marta Pachocka. (2019). "Inventing the Muslim Other in Poland (and Why Does It Differ from Western Europe)". in *Muslim Minorities and the Refugee Crisis in Europe*, edited by K. Górak-Sosnowska, M. Pachocka, and J. Misiuna. Warsaw: SGH Publishing House.

Goździak, Elżbieta M., and Izabella Main. (2020). "European Norms and Values and the Refugee Crisis: Issues and Challenges". Pp. 1–11 in *Europe and the Refugee Response: A Crisis of Values?*, Routledge Studies in Development, Displacement and Resettlement, edited by E. M. Goździak, I. Main, and B. Suter. New York: Routledge.

Goździak, Elżbieta M., and Brigitte Suter. (2020). "Concluding Thoughts". Pp. 59–73 in *Europe and the Refugee Response: A Crisis of Values?*, Routledge Studies in Development, Displacement and Resettlement, edited by E. M. Goździak, I. Main, and B. Suter. New York: Routledge.

Green, Emma. (2017). "How Marine Le Pen Uses Christianity as an Argument against Islam in Secular France". *The Atlantic*. Viewed from: www.theatlantic.com/international/archive/2017/05/christian-identity-france/525558/ [Date accessed: 17 September 2024].

Hadas, Edward. (2020). *Counsels of Imperfection: Thinking through Catholic Social Teaching*. Washington, DC: CUA Press.

Hefele, Karl Joseph von. (1860). *The Life of Cardinal Ximenez*. Catholic Publishing & Bookselling Company.

Heimburger, Robert W. (2018). *God and the Illegal Alien: United States Immigration Law and a Theology of Politics*. Cambridge: Cambridge University Press.

Hoffmeier, James. (2009). *The Immigration Crisis: Immigrants, Aliens, and the Bible*. Wheaton: Crossway.

Hollenbach, SJ, David. (2019). *Humanity in Crisis: Ethical and Religious Response to Refugees*. Washington, DC: Georgetown University Press.

Holy and Great Council. (2016). "Encyclical of the Holy Council of the Orthodox Church". Viewed from: https://holycouncil.org/encyclical-holy-council [Date accessed: 18 December 2024].

Hoppe, Leslie J. (2007). "Israel and Egypt: Relationships and Memory". *The Bible Today* 45.

In Context. (2022). "'We Will Not Receive Even One Muslim' – Polish Politician on Refugees". March 22. Viewed from: www.youtube.com/watch?v=lf5QYD9njrk [Date accessed: 28 August 2024].

Jaskulowski, Krzysztof. (2019). *The Everyday Politics of Migration Crisis in Poland: Between Nationalism, Fear and Empathy*. Cham: Springer International Publishing.

Jenrick, Robert. (2024). "The Attitudes of Our Establishment Have Weakened English Identity". *Mail Online*, September 19. Viewed from: www.dailymail.co.uk/debate/article-/attitudes-policies-metropolitan-establishment-English-identity-England risk-Robert.html [Date accessed: 20 September 2024].

Kamen, Henry. (2014). *The Spanish Inquisition: A Historical Revision.* Yale University Press.

Katanacho, Yohanna. (2005). "Christ Is the Owner of Haaretz". *Christian Scholar's Review* 34(4):425–41.

Koehler, L., W. Baumgartner, M. E. J. Richardson, and J. J. Stamm. (2000). "גֵּר". *Hebrew and Aramaic Lexicon of the Old Testament* 201.

Krotofil, Joanna, and Dominika Motak. (2018). "Between Traditionalism, Fundamentalism, and Populism: A Critical Discourse Analysis of the Media Coverage of the Migration Crisis in Poland". Pp. 61–85 in *Religion in the European Refugee Crisis*, edited by U. Schmiedel and G. Smith. Cham: Springer International Publishing.

Ladini, Riccardo, Ferruccio Biolcati, Francesco Molteni, Andrea Pedrazzani, and Cristiano Vezzoni. (2021). "The Multifaceted Relationship between Individual Religiosity and Attitudes toward Immigration in Contemporary Italy". *International Journal of Sociology* 51(5):390–411.

LBC. (2024). "Richard Dawkins: I'm a Cultural Christian". April 1. Viewed from: www.youtube.com/watch?v=COHgEFUFWyg [Date accessed: 18 September 2024].

Leuștean, Lucian. (2019). *Forced Migration and Human Security in the Eastern Orthodox World.* 1st ed. Routledge.

Linde, Stig, and Roberto Scaramuzzino. (2018). "Is the Church of Sweden an 'Ordinary' Civil Society Organization?: The Advocacy Activities of the Church in Comparison to Other Civil Society Organizations in Sweden". *Nordic Journal of Religion and Society* 31(2):118–38.

Mattei, Roberto De. (2021). *Saint Pius V: The Legendary Pope Who Excommunicated Queen Elizabeth I, Standardized the Mass, and Defeated the Ottoman Empire.* Sophia Institute Press.

Mazurczak, Filip. (2018). "Poland's Christian Migrants". *First Things*, July 20. Viewed from: www.firstthings.com/web-exclusives/2018/07/polands-christian-migrants [Date accessed: 17 September 2024].

McDaniel, Eric Leon, Irfan Nooruddin, and Allyson Faith Shortle. (2011). "Divine Boundaries: How Religion Shapes Citizens' Attitudes toward Immigrants". *American Politics Research* 39(1):205–33.

Melkonian-Hoover, Ruth M., and Lyman A. Kellstedt. (2019). *Evangelicals and Immigration: Fault Lines among the Faithful.* Cham: Springer International Publishing.

Moreland, J. P. (2013). "A Biblical Case for Limited Government". Viewed from: https://ifwe.wpenginepowered.com/wp-content/uploads/2013/04/A-Biblical-Case-for-Limited-Government-Moreland.pdf [Date accessed: 18 December 2024].

Nanko-Fernández, Carmen M. (2015). "A 'Documented' Response: Papal Teaching and People on the Move". Pp. 1–21 in *Immigrant Neighbors among Us: Immigration across Theological Traditions*, edited by M. D. C. R. and L. A. Sánchez M. Eugene: Pickwick Publications.

The Newsmakers. (2019). "Here's Why Poland Takes in Millions of Migrants . . . Just Not Muslim Ones". April 2. Viewed from: www.youtube.com/watch?v=TYSX2vI7oPk [Date accessed: 18 September 2024].

Orlinsky, Harry M. (1986). "The Biblical Concept of the Land of Israel: Cornerstone of the Covenant between God and Israel". Pp. 27–64 in *The Land of Israel: Jewish Perspectives, Studies in Judaism and Christianity in Antiquity*, edited by L. A. Hoffman. South Bend: University of Notre Dame Press.

Paul II, John. (2001). "Message for the 87th World Day of Migration". Viewed from: https://www.vatican.va/content/john-paul-/en/messages/migration/documents/hf_jp-ii_mes_20010213_world-migration-day-2001.html [Date accessed: 14 July 2025].

Peppiatt, Lucy. (2022). *The Imago Dei: Humanity Made in the Image of God.* Cascade Books.

Pérez, Joseph. (2007). *History of a Tragedy: The Expulsion of the Jews from Spain.* Urbana: University of Illinois Press.

Poliakov, Léon. (1965). *The History of Anti-Semitism.* Vol. 1. London: Elek Books.

Roy, Olivier. (2018). "'A Kitsch Christianity': Populists Gather Support While Traditional Religiosity Declines". *Religion and Global Society.* Viewed from: https://blogs.lse.ac.uk/religionglobalsociety/2018/10/a-kitsch-christianity-populists-gather-support-while-traditional-religiosity-declines/ [Date accessed: 17 September 2024].

Sessions, Jeff. (2018). "Attorney General Sessions Addresses Recent Criticisms of Zero Tolerance by Church Leaders". *U.S. Department of Justice | Office of Public Affairs.* Viewed from: www.justice.gov/opa/speech/attorney-general-sessions-addresses-recent-criticisms-zero-tolerance-church-leaders [Date accessed: 21 February 2024].

Shakeshaft, Paul. (2024). "Richard Dawkins, Cultural Christian". *First Things*, July 2. Viewed from: www.firstthings.com/web-exclusives/2024/07/richard-dawkins-cultural-christian [Date accessed: 18 September 2024].

Snyder, Susanna. (2012). *Asylum-Seeking, Migration and Church*. London: Ashgate.
Soerens, Matthew, and Jenny Yang. (2009). *Welcoming the Stranger: Justice, Compassion & Truth in the Immigration Debate*. Downers Grove, IL: IVP Books.
Stackhouse, John G. (2022). *Evangelicalism: A Very Short Introduction*. Oxford University Press.
Stow, Kenneth R. (1977). *Catholic Thought and Papal Jewry Policy, 1555–1593*. New York: Jewish Theological Seminary of America.
Stow, Kenneth R. (1992). "The Papacy and the Jews: Catholic Reformation and Beyond". *Jewish History* 6(1/2):257–79.
Stow, Kenneth R. (2015). "More Than Meets the Eye: Pius V and the Jews". Pp. 375–94 in *Dominikaner und Juden/Dominicans and Jews: Personen, Konflikte und Perspektiven vom 13. bis zum 20. Jahrhundert/Personalities, Conflicts, and Perspectives from the 13th to the 20th Century*, edited by E. H. Füllenbach and G. Miletto. De Gruyter (A).
Strand, Daniel. (2015). "Throwing Caution to the Wind: Charity and the Dilemma of America's Syrian Immigration Policy". *Providence*, November 25. Viewed from: https://providencemag.com/2015/11/response-responsibility-a-symposium-on-the-syrian-refugee-crisis/#throwingcaution [Date accessed: 31 May 2021].
Stroope, Samuel, Heather M. Rackin, and Paul Froese. (2021). "Christian Nationalism and Views of Immigrants in the United States: Is the Relationship Stronger for the Religiously Inactive?" *Socius* 7.
Suter, Brigitte, and Roberto Scaramuzzino. (2020). "Abolishing Asylum and Violating the Human Rights of Refugees: Why Is It Tolerated?: The Case of Hungary in the EU". Pp. 59–73 in *Europe and the Refugee Response: A Crisis of Values?, Routledge Studies in Development, Displacement and Resettlement*, edited by E. M. Goździak, I. Main, and B. Suter. New York: Routledge.
Swain, Carol M. (2011). "A Judeo-Christian Approach to 'Comprehensive' Immigration Reform". *The Review of Faith & International Affairs* 9(1):11–15.
Terpstra, Nicholas. (2015). *Religious Refugees in the Early Modern World: An Alternative History of the Reformation*. Cambridge: Cambridge University Press.
Today News. (2022). "Rwandan Anglican Archbishop Defends UK Asylum Plan". Viewed from: https://web.archive.org/web/

20220618135317/www.today.ng/news/africa/rwandananglican-archbishop-defends-asylum-plan-430242 [Date accessed: 1 April 2024].

van Selm, Joanne. (2020). "Community-Based Sponsorship of Refugees Resettling in the UK British Values in Action?" Pp. 59–73 in *Europe and the Refugee Response: A Crisis of Values?, Routledge Studies in Development, Displacement and Resettlement*, edited by E. M. Goździak, I. Main, and B. Suter. New York: Routledge.

Vidalon, Dominique, and Gonzalo Fuentes. (2024). "France's Far-Right RN Makes Immigration Pillar of Europe Poll Campaign". *Reuters*, March 4. Viewed from: www.reuters.com/world/europe/frances-far-right-rn-makes-immigration-pillar-europe-poll-campaign-2024-03-03/ [Date accessed: 20 September 2024].

Walls, Andrew F. (1996). *Missionary Movement in Christian History: Studies in the Transmission of Faith*. Orbis Books.

Wielenga, Bob. (2020). "The Gēr [Immigrant] in Postexilic Prophetic Eschatology: The Perspectives of Ezekiel 47:22–23 and Malachi 3:5". *In Die Skriflig/In Luce Verbi* 54(1):9.

Wilczyńska, Anna, and Karol Wilczyński. (2020). "In Poland the Stranger Threatens Christianity: Polish Catholics and Their Attitude towards Refugees". Pp. 91–102 in *Cosmopolitanism, Migration and Universal Human Rights*, edited by M. C. Jacobsen, E. Berhanu Gebre, and D. Župarić-Iljić. Cham: Springer International Publishing.

Williams, Hattie. (n.d.). "Rwanda Bill Is Immoral and Unworkable, Bishops Tell Government". Viewed from: www.churchtimes.co.uk/articles/2024/2-february/news/uk/rwanda-bill-is-immoral-and-unworkable-bishops-tell-government [Date accessed: 1 April 2024].

Wodak, Ruth. (2022). "Entering the 'Post-Shame Era': The Rise of Illiberal Democracy, Populism and Neo-Authoritarianism in Europe". in *The Limits of Europe: Identities, Spaces, Values*, edited by R. Foster and J. Grzymski. Bristol: Bristol University Press.

Wolfe, Stephen. (2022). *The Case for Christian Nationalism*. Moscow, ID: Canon Press.

Wormald, Benjamin. (2015). "Chapter 1: The Changing Religious Composition of the U.S." *Pew Research Center*. Viewed from: www.pewresearch.org/religion/2015/05/12/chapter-1-the-changing-religious-composition-of-the-u-s/ [Date accessed: 26 March 2025].

Wright, Christopher J. H. (2004). *Old Testament Ethics for the People of God*. Downers Grove, IL: Inter-Varsity Press.

Zehnder, Markus. (2021). *The Bible and Immigration: A Critical and Empirical Reassessment*. Wipf and Stock Publishers.

Zurlo, Gina A., Todd M. Johnson, and Peter F. Crossing. (2022). "World Christianity and Religions 2022: A Complicated Relationship". *International Bulletin of Mission Research* 46(1):71–80.

3
A JEWISH CASE STUDY

Judaism, as a religious resource influencing how Jews address immigration, offers a unique case study. This chapter will compare the policies of the sovereign Jewish-dominated State of Israel and those of the small, ethno-religious Jewish minority in the United States. Of course, both communities share sacred texts, a memory of the long period of exile/diaspora and oppression, and behavioral expectations that derive from religious traditions. American Jews feel a deep connection to Israel (in a 2021 Pew survey, only 16% claimed little connection to Israel, while 88% claimed a great deal or some connection – Nortey 2021), yet their unique experience in the United States provides a helpful contrast to Jews in the State of Israel, allowing us to explore the different ways that Judaism directs both religious values and behaviors in the twenty-first century. This case study will offer competing views on immigration, with special reference to how to treat refugees and those who are not Jewish.

As noted in the introduction, religion is expressed with both dimensions of religious identity that often include shared values, on the one hand, and expected behavioral norms that result from belief and practice, on the other hand. Judaism, with its strong tradition of *halakhic* expectation and of legally binding demands, has much to say about what a Jew should do; ironically, because of its structure of law, Judaism historically often had little to say about values that may underlie the law and its behavioral expectations. One approach to expected Jewish behavior simply states, "The value of a *mitzvah* – following any

DOI: 10.4324/9781032645209-4

particular commandment – is to do another *mitzvah*" (Mishnah Avot 4:2). No other reason or justification for following the rules is necessary; ritually mandated behavior need make no rational or ethical demand. While Jewish religious observance in Israel runs the gamut from atheist to fervent ultra-Orthodox, strict religious law is often government policy due to the inclusion of Orthodox political parties in the governing coalition.

Yet, as we have seen in the contemporary period, a greater focus on Jewish values has come forward, one of which states that Jews must be partnering with God in repairing the world. That is most evident in the American Jewish community, where there is no legal or political mechanism to enforce any Jewish behavior. Also noted in the abovementioned Pew study, ritual behavior for American Jews rates very low compared to living an ethical life, fighting for greater social and economic justice, and even having a good sense of humor.

The distinctive ways that each community addresses immigration offer great insight into how a religious community can engage text and tradition to support very different policies. We will first address the policies and Jewish voices of the sovereign State of Israel and then the policy statements and Jewish voices of Jewish organizations in the United States.

The State of Israel Is Unique

In what most, if not all, Jews considered a miracle following the catastrophe of the Holocaust, the nascent UN endorsed a Jewish state in part of what had been the British mandate for Palestine. As stated in the Israeli Declaration of Independence, open immigration became policy, but only for a specific group: "The State of Israel will be open for Jewish immigration and for the Ingathering of the Exiles." (Israel State Archives). The implementation of this policy mimicked Nazi law concerning who was to be considered a Jew. This meant that anyone born to a Jewish parent or grandparent as well as the one who converted, the spouse, or a child or parent of a Jew, would be welcomed. Others were not invited to join, and the process of becoming a citizen, if at all allowed, would be onerous. Israel was meant to be more than a haven. Its purpose was to create a Jewish culture, a Jewish society whose norms, values, traditions, and customs would reflect a uniquely Jewish identity. Its justification was written into its Declaration of Independence:

> In the year 1897 the first Zionist Congress, inspired by Theodore Herzl's vision of a Jewish state, proclaimed the right of the Jewish people to a national revival in their own country. This right was acknowledged by the Balfour Declaration of November 2, 1917, and reaffirmed by the mandate of the League of Nations, which gave explicit international recognition to the historic connection of the Jewish people with Palestine and their right to reconstitute their national home.
> *(Foreign Ministry, Israel State Archives)*

What then is an authentic Israeli and who is foreign in the Jewish state? We will address the specific strategies Israeli policymakers use to protect the Jewishness of the state, the one possible case study of how Jews, in their autonomy, deal with those immigrants who do not fall under the categories of the Law of Return.

In Israel today, where Jews are a majority and empowered to determine policy, a significant cohort harks back to the Bible's exhortation to wipe out impurities in the land. Those who call for the expulsion of Palestinians, who burn down their olive orchards, threaten and assault Palestinians, and, in extreme cases, murder as well, cite specific biblical verses fortified by rabbinic statements both centuries old and contemporary. Government policy in recent years demanded that African asylum seekers must be expelled, sent somewhere in Africa, and removed from the sacred soil of the Land of Israel. While ostensibly on the periphery of Israeli politics, in 2022, political parties espousing exclusionary and violent policies against those who are not Jewish entered the governing coalition. These parties offer both religious and demographic justifications for the policies they have or seek to enact. We will explore both.

In the early years following independence, Israel brought in refugees from European DP camps as well as those fleeing Middle East and North African Muslim countries. In the first 20 years, the Jewish population increased by two million. With immigration from countries in the Soviet sphere between 1990 and 2005, the population again increased by almost one and a half million. In that sense, Israeli governments supported immigration from around the world as long as it fit the Law of Return criterion established in 1950 that anyone with a Jewish grandparent or married to a Jew would be welcomed as a citizen. Yet this immigration policy, because it allowed non-Jewish relatives to settle in Israel according to the Law of Return, meant that by 2021, 42% of those immigrating were not Jewish according to the Ministry of Religion. As in many places around the world where ethnic or religious purity is central to political debate, the presence of non-Jewish immigrants caused a strong negative reaction among some elements of the nation about diluting the Jewish majority. For example, the right-wing NGO Israeli Immigration Policy Center stated

> While the Israeli government approves hasty decisions in favor of increasing the non-Jewish population, the results of the perforated policy are already clear. . . . Four out of five Israelis who move abroad are Jewish, whereas two out of five immigrants to Israel are non-Jewish. We will continue to work to ensure the future of Israel as a Jewish and democratic state.
> *(Greenwood 2022)*

In fact, over the decades since independence, the Jewish majority dropped from almost 90% in the 1950s to approximately 73% by 2024. The anxiety of a demographic loss of the Jewish majority certainly influences Israeli policymakers and key elements of the population. This has led to a range of laws and policies that assert the primacy of Jewish identity, from language to culture to national mission, and the exclusion, where possible, of those who do not so identify.

In Israel, where Orthodox Jewish law can be enforced by the state, rabbis have great political power as members of the governing coalition. Jewish law, backed by the state, is used to sanction such things as marriage and divorce, child custody, what transportation can run on the Sabbath, and who is included as an authentic Jew. It comes as no surprise that Jewish law and tradition are involved in determining policies affecting immigration, inclusion, and acceptance or rejection of foreigners into Israel. Rabbis will have an authoritative Jewish voice on how to deal with those not automatically welcomed based on the Law of Return. In Israel, on the spectrum of religious observance, the form of Judaism that dominates politically is Judaism understood as a set of commandments to be followed according to Jewish law.

The rigidly Orthodox Haredi (literally, those who "quake") community in Israel rejects even many of those who identify as Jews but do not meet the extreme demands of Haredi rabbis. For these fervent believers, even allowing such self-identifying Jews to live in Israel is a concession. This has included Jews converted by non-Orthodox rabbis and Jews from India and Ethiopia. Over the decades of Israel's existence, political leaders of the Haredi community have held many positions within the governing coalitions. There is no welcome for those they consider strangers.

The ultra-Orthodox view of the coalition was well expressed by the former Chief Rabbi Ovadia Yosef (1920–2013), who was also the spiritual guide of a powerful political party. He explained that the Torah promoted laws to live by, not die by, so saving a life takes precedence over all the laws in the Torah. Yet he then went on to explain that this applies only to saving a Jewish life. He forbade a Jew to desecrate the Sabbath to save the life of a Gentile (Zeiger 2012).

While represented in the Knesset by political parties such as Shas and United Torah Judaism, the ultra-Orthodox rabbis have influence but have not been able to impose their more stringent views on immigration policy.

Another view on non-Jews in Israel and who belongs is found in the religious Zionists who create settlements on the West Bank and try to expel Palestinians from their land in the hope that they will emigrate. An extreme example of this political stance occurred in 1994 when Baruch Goldstein left a Jewish holiday Purim service in which biblical passages were read that called for the God-commanded annihilation of the ancient, long-ago extinct tribe of Amalek (a biblical adversary of the Israelites as they were in the desert leaving Egypt) and proceeded to murder 29 Muslims who were in prayer. His grave remains a pilgrimage site for a segment of the Jewish population of Israel and beyond. Symbolically, there is no better example of the impact of millennia-old religious texts on the contemporary attitudes and actions of a significant percentage of Israeli Jews.

What the religious and nonreligious coalition partners share is a negative attitude toward the Palestinian population. This is the one area, centering on Palestinians, where there is public debate across all political parties and viewpoints with a wide range of viewpoints. The most recent example of policy proposals to expel Palestinians came from government ministers during the war with Hamas. National Security Minister Itamar Ben-Gvir stated that "We must promote a solution to encourage the emigration of the residents of Gaza." This was followed by Finance Minister Bezalel Smotrich, who demanded that Gazans be expelled so that Israelis could settle and make the desert bloom (France 2024). While gaining media coverage, such a policy of expulsion is at this time opposed by both the Cabinet and the majority of the Knesset.

A different complicated example is the government policy toward Eritrean and other East African asylum seekers passed in 2018. While Israel, following international practice, accepts as asylum seekers those refugees fleeing violence and death threats, the government, pressured by those wanting to expel foreigners, lifted any limitations on the length of detention. Later, the Israeli Supreme Court decided to accept a government plan to deport African asylum seekers without consent to be sent to "safe third countries" such as Rwanda and Uganda, places with which these refugees may have no relationship (Cesana 2018).

Many asylum seekers, among them survivors of torture, resisted deportation. Riots ensued, and over 100,000 Israeli Jews as well as African migrants protested, while Jewish Israeli refugee rights groups condemned the government's actions.

The Israeli government, led by its right-wing cabinet ministers, called for stringent and extralegal action to detain and expel refugees involved in protests and riots, a policy supported by two-thirds of Israelis (Altman 2018). Yet the situation remains in flux, given the security concerns and war of 2023–2025. The Israeli government of Bibi Netanyahu reflects both the nationalist views that challenge accepting immigrants and the views of the ultra-Orthodox and religious Zionists who are part of the governing coalition.

Interestingly, while Israel is deeply divided in so many ways, there have been no riots or even demonstrations demanding that Israel block immigration. There is no political party formed specifically as anti-immigrant. The question of who should be allowed to live in Israel is not a salient or compelling issue except in reference to Palestinians.

In fact, many Israelis come to the defense of refugees. There is a vibrant coalition of remarkable civil and human rights organizations that seek to protect non-Jews even beyond Palestinians, such as foreign domestic and agricultural workers, from legal or social exclusion and expulsion. There are groups that will stand with Palestinians when they are attacked by Jewish thugs trying to force them out of their villages. *Tag Meir* – a Jewish response to those who burn down Arab olive orchards – comes the next day to replant trees. Wahat al-Salam/Neve Shalom is a cohabitation village of Jews and Palestinians that models care and coexistence at a time when government ministers call for the expulsion of Arabs.

Civil society in Israel is vibrant, and the Aid Organization for Refugees and Asylum Seekers in Israel (ASSAF) serves as an umbrella organization for much of the progressive coalition in Israel. It responded on behalf of Israeli Jews who deplore the government's attempts to expel refugees:

> Anyone who was surprised by the barrage of populist statements that came out of the cabinet, and who expected otherwise, are naïve. . . . The government is proposing to use anti-democratic practices such as administrative, thereby paving the way for another fatal violation of (refugee) human rights and is trying to prepare public opinion for further legislation that will harm them and lead to persecution and systematic harassment.
>
> *(Liss 2023)*

As of this moment, no legislation barring asylum seekers and refugees has been passed.

Among the Nations: The Jewish Minority in the United States

For most Jews, identity in the diaspora, unconstrained by rabbinic authority, is less a function of ritual behaviors than attitudes and meaning that derive from values perhaps unique to their place as a fragile minority. American Jews overwhelmingly support increased human and civil rights. In spite of traditional Orthodox views, for example, 77% of Jews support same-sex marriage and 83% support a woman's right to determine abortion. American Jewish views on immigration are similarly liberal. In 2020, the Times of Israel, citing an American Jewish Committee survey that 75% of Jews opposed Donald Trump's immigration policies, noted that "Fueled by an awareness of their roots as perpetual refugees and recent immigrants, American Jews have long been at the forefront of immigration advocacy in the United States" (Campeas 2020).

Where rabbis have no civic authority, what Jewish law has to say must conform to the values that American Jews cherish. When it does, Jewish texts and traditions will be employed to justify the policy statements of Jewish organizations. When the tradition does not conform, as with homosexuality or how Jews are to view their non-Jewish neighbors, then the law will be repudiated, and history or alternative values will ground the decisions.

Jews in the United States are a fractional minority; their circumstances are radically different than in Israel, where Jews are the majority and have power over who is allowed in and who will be barred from entrance to the Jewish state. Whereas ethnic and religious Jewish cultural supremacy is valued in Israel, in the diaspora, the acceptance of Jews as part of a multiethnic nation gains greater significance. Kevin MacDonald notes that

> Jews have [had] an interest in opposing the establishment of ethnically and culturally homogeneous societies in which they reside as minorities. Jews have been at the forefront in supporting movements aimed at altering the ethnic status quo in the United States in favor of immigration of non-European peoples.

These activities have involved leadership in Congress, organizing and funding anti-restrictionist groups composed of Jews and Gentiles, and originating intellectual movements opposed to evolutionary and biological perspectives in the social sciences.

(MacDonald 1998)

In fact, so clear is the Jewish stance on what America should be that conspiracy theorists see this commitment to immigration and cultural diversity as a Jewish threat. From Hungary to the United States, Jews such as George Soros are accused of promoting "Replacement Theory," undermining the dominance of the Christian nation.

So the commandment to care for the stranger has grown in meaning and scope. A former Orthodox Chief Rabbi of the United Kingdom could write:

What is hard is to love the stranger, one whose color, culture or creed is different from yours. That is why the command, "Love the stranger because you were once strangers," resonates so often throughout the Bible. It is summoning us now. A bold act of collective generosity will show that the world, particularly Europe, has learned the lesson of its own dark past and is willing to take a global lead in building a more hopeful future. Wars that cannot be won by weapons can sometimes be won by the sheer power of acts of humanitarian generosity to inspire the young to choose the way of peace instead of holy war.

(Sachs 2019)

In the most contemporary read of the Torah text of care for the stranger, the awareness of Jewish obligation is articulated as part of a global commandment to be partners with God – *shutafim haKadosh Baruch Hu* – which will bring about *Tikkun Olam*, the repair of the world. For Jews, there is no theology without history, the lived experience of Jews over thousands of years of exile, assault, and navigating their relationship with the places in which they lived. That is why the union of text and history is often cited as an overarching command (Elcott 1995). As Rabbi Reuven Firestone, an American professor, notes:

> We live today in a world of many nations that treat their strangers – their minorities – as the ancient Egyptians treated our ancestors in Egypt. In rare occasions, oppression is relieved by the direct and miraculous power of the Creator. More often, oppression is relieved in other ways: through the grace of God's likeness in the faces of helping neighbors – or helping strangers. As Jews who know the suffering of the oppressed, we are especially obligated to reach out to the strangers in our midst. And we are equally obligated not to ignore the cry of the oppressed elsewhere, but to welcome those who flee the horrors of tyranny and persecution.
>
> *(Firestone n.d.)*

Because being an ethical human being and working for justice and equality in society far outweigh ritual observance and synagogue attendance for diaspora Jews, the principles surrounding the concept of *Tikkun Olam* motivate much of the North American liberal Jewish community (meaning the great majority that comprises American Jewry) to endorse compassionate and supportive immigration policies. In that sense, the historical experience of Jews in the diaspora has powerfully influenced the choice of biblical texts to apply to civil and human rights policymaking.

In fact, even the Orthodox Union that speaks for the more politically conservative mainstream Orthodox Jewish community of North America could state in a 2015 press release during a debate over immigration policy:

> The Jewish community has an important perspective on this debate. Just a few decades ago, refugees from the terror and violence in Hitler's Europe sought refuge in the United States and were turned away due to suspicions about their nationality. In fact, the Jewish immigrants that ultimately came to these shores fully adopted American values and have contributed greatly to the fabric of our great nation of immigrants. Thus, we encourage a sensible process of reviewing and enhancing

security. Neither partisan politics nor xenophobia can have a place in that debate.

The examples of pro-immigration attitudes among American Jews are compelling. The HIAS is the American Jewish organization that represents the Jewish community on issues of immigration. Its mission statement, proclaimed on its website, explains, "Drawing on our Jewish values and history, HIAS provides vital services to refugees and asylum seekers around the world and advocates for their fundamental rights so they can rebuild their lives." This is fortified by many Jewish organizations such as the Reform Movement's Religious Action Center statement found on its advocacy website:

> Our own people's history as "strangers" reminds us of the many struggles faced by immigrants today, and we affirm our commitment to create the same opportunities for today's immigrants that were so valuable to our own community not so many years ago.

Even the risk-averse Jewish Federation of North America (JFNA), which represents 350 Jewish communities from every state, adds "supporting refugees fleeing persecution" to its mission (JFNA 2022). Multiple Jewish organizations representing most of the organizational American Jewish community are founders and engaged members of the Interfaith Immigration Coalition. In the last major effort to reform the immigration policies of the United States, they were vocal advocates of a more welcoming approach to immigration (Elcott).

In the past years, there have been Jewish voices in the United States that oppose immigration (e.g., a survey found that 84% of Haredi ultra-Orthodox voters reported having voted for Trump in 2020, tacitly supporting his anti-immigrant stance) (Sharon, J.). But those voices are not reflected in the official policies of any major Jewish organization nor do affect Jewish voting or attitudes. While Stephen Miller, whose family came as Jewish refugees, may have been the Jewish architect of President Trump's "zero-immigration" policies, over 75% of American Jews opposed those policies and supported more lenient immigration reform

(Kampeas 2020). When 150,000 undocumented immigrants were shipped to New York City in 2022, over 36 synagogues, organizations, and Jewish aid agencies mobilized to provide support. Supporting more liberal immigration seems to have become a contemporary commandment.

Conclusion

What we have shown is the complexity of applying religious traditions to contemporary policies. In these two case studies that explore the impact of Jewish religious texts, values, and traditions on refugee and asylum immigration policies, we see the many ways that religion has a direct impact on Jewish lobbying, advocacy, government laws, and policies. Ancient texts are applied to global affairs, values debated for millennia resurface to explain and justify policy decisions. Prayers are reinterpreted and invoked to call on compassion and acceptance of "the stranger in our midst," while others fortify the demand for Jewish exclusive exceptionalism to protect the Jewish identity of Israel. If anyone doubts the deep and expanding relationship between religion and politics in the twenty-first century, Jewish attitudes and policies concerning immigration offer clear testimony to the contrary. The exploration of this nexus of faith and politics is key to understanding much of immigration policies around the world.

References

Altman, Yair. (2018). "Israel Jews Support Government Policy to Deport Africans". *Israel HaYom*. Viewed from: www.israelhayom.com/2018/02/08/66-of-israeli-jews-support-government-policy-to-deport-africans/ [Date accessed: 24 October 2024].

Campeas, Ron. (2020). "Trumps Policy Is Working against Him". *Times of Israel*. Viewed from: www.timesofisrael.com/for-most-us-jews-trumps-immigration-policy-is-working-against-him/ [Date accessed: 24 October 2024].

Cesana, Shlomo. (2018). "Israel Gives Illegal Immigrants 3 Months". *Israel HaYom*. Viewed from: www.israelhayom.com/2018/01/03/israel-gives-illegal-migrants-3-months-to-leave-or-face-jail/ [Date accessed: 24 October 2024].

Elcott, David. (1995). *A Sacred Journey*. New York: Rowman & Littlefield.
Firestone, Reuven. (n.d.). "Reform Judaism". Viewed from: https://reformjudaism.org/learning/torah-study/torah-commentary/commandment-love-and-help-stranger [Date accessed: 24 October 2024].
France 24. (2024). "U.S. Condemns Far-Right Israeli Ministers". Viewed from: www.france24.com/en/middle-east/20240103-us-condemns-far-right-israeli-ministers-call-for-palestinians-to-emigrate-from-gaza [Date accessed: 24 October 2024].
Greenwood, Hanan. (2022). "Immigrants to Israel". Viewed from: www.israelhayom.com/2022/01/13/42-of-immigrants-to-israel-in-2021-are-non-jews-cbs-finds/ [Date accessed: 24 October 2024].
Israel State Archives. (1948). "Declaration of Independence". Viewed from: "The State of Israel Will Be Open for Jewish immigration and for the Ingathering of the Exiles." (Israel State Archives. [Date accessed: 24 October 2024].
JFNA. (n.d.). Viewed from: https://cdn.fedweb.org/fed-42/2/Jewish%2520Federations%25202023%2520Policy%2520Priorities.pdf [Date accessed: 24 October 2024].
Kampeas, Ron. (2020). "For American Jews Immigration Looms Large". Viewed from: www.jta.org/2020/11/03/politics/for-american-jews-immigration-looms-large-in-the-voting-booth-and-they-dont-like-what-trump-has-done [Date accessed: 24 October 2024].
Liss, Jonathan. (2023). "Israeli Government Plans to Hold Arrested Asylum Seekers". Viewed from: www.haaretz.com/israel-news/2023-09-03/ty-article/.premium/israeli-govt-plans-to-hold-arrested-asylum-seekers-without-trial-sources-say/0000018a-5ac6-d0ea-a7ab-daefb6da0000 [Date accessed: 24 October 2024].
MacDonald, K. (1998). "Jewish Involvement in Shaping Immigration Policy 1881–1965: A Historical Review". *Population and Environment* 19.
Mishnah Avot. (1964). *Pirkei Avot 4:2*. New York: Judaica Press.
Nortey, Justin. (2021). "U.S. Jews Have Widely Different Views on Israel". *Pew Research Center*. Viewed from: www.pewresearch.org/short-reads/2021/05/21/u-s-jews-have-widely-differing-views-on-israel/ [Date accessed: 24 October 2024].
Orthodox Union. (2015). "Press Release". Viewed from: https://advocacy.ou.org/orthodox-union-statement-regarding-syrian-refugees-issue/ [Date accessed: 24 October 2024].

Sachs, Jonathan. (2019). "Loving the Stranger". Viewed from: https://blogs.timesofisrael.com/loving-the-stranger-mishpatim-5779/ [Date accessed: 24 October 2024].

Sharon, Jeremy. (2020). "Why Are so Many Orthodox Jews Voting for Trump". Viewed from: www.jpost.com/us-elections/why-are-so-many-orthodox-jews-voting-for-trump-analysis-647681 [Date accessed: 24 October 2024].

Zeiger, Asher. (2012). "Ovadia Yosef Speaks Out". Viewed from: www.timesofisrael.com/ovadia-yosef-speaks-against-sabbath-desecration-to-save-non-jewish-lives/ [Date accessed: 18 December 2024].

4
A CHRISTIAN CASE STUDY: THE 2015 REFUGEE "CRISIS"

Introduction

The year 2015 witnessed over a million refugees and migrants crossing into Europe from oppressed and war-torn contexts. European nations responded in diverse ways falling into two broad categories: (1) reinforcing borders in alarm and (2) opening borders in welcome. The polar extremes of these responses are represented by two figures: Viktor Orbán, the prime minister of Hungary, and Angela Merkel, the chancellor of Germany. Where Orbán built a fence at Hungary's border to keep the migrants out and proclaimed a policy of zero acceptance, Merkel opened Germany's borders wide, allowing more than a million Syrian refugees to enter.

This chapter contends that *both* Orbán's and Merkel's responses were religiously motivated but drew on different aspects of Christianity. These two aspects correspond to the two meanings of religion we identified in the Introduction. Orbán was concerned with preserving Christianity as a communal identity and protecting Hungarian culture from Muslim influence. Merkel's posture of radical welcome drew on Christianity as belief and practice, manifesting a commitment to social justice and solidarity with the poor and disadvantaged.

A Brief Sketch of Events

The whole sequence of events has come to be known as the European refugee crisis. However, this name arguably shifts attention from the plight of the refugees to that of the host nations (see Schmiedel & Smith 2018: 4). We will call it instead the Syrian refugee crisis. The Syrian civil war started in 2011, and by 2015, more than ten million Syrians had fled their homes to escape persecution or death. Most went to neighboring nations like Jordan or Lebanon, but some traveled further. Next to Afghans, Iraqis, and others fleeing similar situations, they traipsed across Turkey, passed through Greece and Serbia, and joined the flow of Kosovars trying to enter the Schengen area.

The Schengen area is a region of Europe without any border controls. Anyone inside can travel from one country to another unchecked. The politicians who established it in 1999 were thinking of freedom of movement for EU citizens. For refugees, there was a different protocol: the Dublin regulation, which stated that an asylum seeker must remain in the first safe country in which they arrived. If they are found in another country, they are sent back to that first country of entry in order to have their asylum claim assessed. The Schengen/Dublin policy combination had seemed reasonable enough when it was agreed, but in the context of mass immigration, it was shown to place an unfair burden on countries with an outer border to the Schengen area.

Hungary was the outer border of the Schengen area on the refugee route from Turkey and Greece. By May 2015, 400 people a day were crossing the border into Hungary. According to the Dublin regulation, they were supposed to remain there. But Hungary was a comparatively poor nation in the Schengen area, and the absence of border controls meant that there was no *practical* obstacle to free movement to other Schengen nations. Hence, most of these asylum seekers intended to pass through Hungary into Western Europe.

On 17 June, the Hungarian government announced that it would build a tall razor-wire fence along its border to stop migrants from entering. This news had the opposite of its intended effect. The refugees felt that it was now or never. They raced to get in before the fence was complete and started to arrive at a rate of more than 2,000 per day. Viktor Orbán said that Hungary would not accept a single one, insisting that they were economic migrants and not genuine refugees (Thorpe 2019: 47, 61). On

23 June, he announced that Hungary was suspending the Dublin regulation.

The Dublin regulation meant different things for different countries. For Hungary, it meant responsibility for the vast majority of asylum seekers trying to enter the Schengen zone. But it did not mean that for Germany. With no Schengen land borders, in theory Germany should have no asylum applications to process. So when, in August 2015, Chancellor Angela Merkel suspended the Dublin regulation for Syrian refugees coming to Germany, the implications were the diametric opposite of Hungary doing the same thing. Effectively, Germany opened the door wide to everyone with a Syrian passport. It did not take long for the news to spread.

Church institutions were quick to issue an urgent appeal to work together in providing support and welcome for the influx of refugees. On 6 September, Pope Francis issued a call to every Catholic parish, religious community, monastery, and sanctuary to provide a home for at least one refugee family (Faiola & Birnbaum 2015). On 9 September, the World Council of Churches, the Conference of European Churches, and the Churches' Commission for Migrants in Europe issued a joint letter urging all church denominations to cooperate in order "to give a common witness of compassion, justice and peace" (World Council of Churches et al. 2015).

Before the end of 2015, over a million asylum seekers had entered Germany, most of whom were from Syria. Germany began the long process of integrating these refugees into German society and the labor market, a process that continues to this day.

Answering the Question "Why?"

These events are well known, yet some of their strangeness may escape us. The question of motivation seems unanswered. Why did Hungary and Germany, Orbán and Merkel, respond in opposite ways to the 2015 refugee influx?

Many scholars explain the responses of Hungary and Germany in ways that omit or minimize the role of religion. Müller-Brandeck-Bocquet (2022: 67–9), for example, has cataloged four explanations for Merkel's actions, none of which mentions her faith or Germany's Christian heritage. Likewise, here are a few other common explanations:

1. Some explain Orbán's and Merkel's actions as an outworking of national self-image informed by history. Hungary had "for centuries . . . self-identified as Europe's bulwark against Muslim conquest" (Betts & Collier 2018: 47). Germany, still living in the shadow of its Nazi past, seized the opportunity to display anti-racist credentials and show itself full of humanitarian impulse.
2. Others give economic explanations. Hungary is a poor nation and did not want the expense of harboring large quantities of refugees. Merkel's welcoming policy was not (or not only) compassionate but "a shrewd long-term economic decision" in the face of Germany's declining and aging population (Bauman et al. 2016: 68).
3. Still others see in these actions a strategic maneuver to please the people and remain in power. Nick Thorpe writes that "after the *Charlie Hebdo* attack [in France], Orbán and his advisers discovered the political value of migrants, or rather the fear of them" (Thorpe 2019: 14). Likewise, Merkel gave in to increasing pressure from the media that was shaping public opinion in favor of the refugees (Kepplinger 2019; cited in Müller-Brandeck-Bocquet 2022: 68).

None of these explanations are wrong *per se*, but insofar as they omit religion, they are not the full story. Religion underlies all of them in various ways. A nation's self-image is bound up with its religious and communal identity, and a politician's strategy must appeal to the values and priorities of the voting public, which have been informed at some level by the nation's religious history. Even economics is based on principles of value that are far from religiously neutral (consider, e.g., the ban on usury common to all the Abrahamic faiths). In what follows, we shall examine the way religious motivations are threaded throughout these two polar-opposite responses to the Syrian refugee crisis, both of which are an outworking of Europe's Christian heritage.

As noted in the Introduction, we cannot naïvely assume that religion is an influence only or even when it is explicit. Orbán was explicit about his Christianity, partly because he knew it would have traction with the people he represented. Merkel, however, did not mention the Christian principles behind her actions for the same reason: it would not have gone down well in largely secular-identifying Germany.

Viktor Orbán and Hungary

It is not about economics. Despite the stated position of Fidesz (Orbán's political party) to accept no immigrants, the Hungarian government has readily accepted two kinds of immigrants: (1) poor Asians, especially Vietnamese, who come to do low-paid jobs that Hungarians do not want to do, filling a gap in the labor market, and (2) wealthy non-Europeans, who until 2017 could obtain permanent residency by buying $322,600 in government bonds. This was an attractive prospect because it was the cheapest way to gain permanent residence inside the Schengen area, and was discontinued because of concerns by other Schengen members. Fidesz is not unaware of immigration's economic benefits.

Nor is it about keeping any and all foreigners out of the country. Immigration in Hungary has never been higher than in the last two years. The number of immigrants in Hungary exceeded 400,000 at the end of 2023, almost double the figure from five years previously (Morina 2024). This is largely due to the number of Ukrainian refugees welcomed into Hungary following the 2022 war in Ukraine. Most of these Ukrainians are Christians, either Catholic or Orthodox.

These unacknowledged exceptions to the "no-immigrant" rule show that what the Hungarian government is opposed to is more precise than immigration as such. Because the above immigrants are not Muslims, they are not viewed as threats to the coherence of Hungarian "Christian" culture.

But Orbán's appeal to Christianity is not simply a political strategy. We will not understand the religious dimension of Hungary's immigration policy if we too quickly categorize Orbán's religion as purely instrumental. Orbán is not simply another Donald

Trump or Marine Le Pen, appealing to religious categories to win votes. His Christian faith appears to be sincere; however, he might also use it for political purpose, and however, one might assess its accuracy in representing Christian ethics.

Like most Hungarians in the Soviet Union, Orbán was raised nonreligious. He and his wife refused to get married in church and instead had a civil wedding in 1986. His party, Fidesz, was initially anticlerical in orientation. His conversion to Christianity was not sudden but gradual. It started when he came under the influence of the Reformed pastor Zoltan Balog. In 1992, after Balog introduced him to some of Hungary's Catholic bishops, he told Balog, "I was not aware that the Church is so important, such an important part of Hungarian life. I cannot talk to the people about politics if I don't understand that!" (cited in Lendvai 2018: 51). In 1996, Balog confirmed him into the Reformed church, and in 1997, he and his wife had a church wedding. When Orbán lost the 2002 election, he refused to be downcast. Instead, he said, "He who carries within him faith, hope and love will see hardships as salvation. . . . Only a person who has lost faith can be vanquished" (cited in Lendvai 2018: 51–2). Then, he led his defeated (and formerly anticlerical) political party in prayer. When Fidesz regained power in 2010, they began to support Hungarian churches in numerous ways.

Orbán's religious convictions, even if genuine, are nonetheless politically expedient and align with Hungary's overall religious attitude, which is why he keeps winning elections. Today, most of Fidesz's leading members are from the Reformed tradition. Reformed Christianity is one of Hungary's two largest religious traditions. To ensure the support of the other, Roman Catholicism, Fidesz maintains a close alliance with the traditionally Catholic party known as the Hungarian Christian Democratic People's Party (KDNP). Some scholars point to the decline in church attendance as evidence that Hungary is largely secular (Ádám & Bozóki 2016; Gallaher & Martin 2020). But to read too much into this would be a mistake, a failure to observe the enduring influence of religion even on secular-identifying people. As we discussed in the Introduction, religious principles can continue to be a driving factor long after someone has ceased religious observance, and religion as communal identity can continue to be important for societies even after their religious principles have eroded. The claim that Hungary is a Christian nation and needs to preserve its Christian values has an appeal beyond regular churchgoers.

Fidesz's turn to religion did not initially come with any particular stance on immigration. Immigration was barely a topic for Orbán or Fidesz before the Syrian refugee crisis and did not feature as a vote-winning strategy until the subsequent election in 2018 (Bender 2020: 61). This is probably because, prior to 2015, Hungary had hardly any immigration requests, so the topic was seen as irrelevant.

But the events of 2015 compelled Orbán and his party to think through the implications of their religion for immigration. Those implications were formulated as the need to preserve Christian European values by keeping Muslims out. Fidesz stated that "the incoming migrants, that were mainly Muslims, will destroy the national and European identities, the culture and the Christian values" (Meszaros 2019: 244). In September 2015, at the height of the Syrian refugee crisis, the Hungarian prime minister said the following in a speech:

> Those arriving have been raised in another religion, and represent a radically different culture. Most of them are not Christians, but Muslims. . . . This is an important question, because Europe and European identity is rooted in Christianity. Is it not worrying in itself that European Christianity is now barely able to keep Europe Christian? There is no alternative, and we have no option but to defend our borders.
> *(cited in Traynor 2015)*

As this quotation shows, Orbán sees not one but two threats to the Europe he seeks to defend. One threat comes from outside, the "invasion" of Muslims that will, he warns, fundamentally alter the Christian culture of Europe. The other threat, alluded to in the last two sentences, is internal: the liberalizing and secularizing trend that undercuts traditional family values and celebrates multiculturalism. This is why Orbán both loves Europe and hates the EU. The former is what he is defending, and the latter is pushing an ideology that will in his view destroy Europe. As one report puts it, Orbán's political party, Fidesz, is

> waging a two-front war: they defend Christian values by fighting against the "Islamization" of Europe, and they protect the traditional values against the liberal, "post-1968" ideologies such as multiculturalism and gender equality, which currently rule the West but at same time undermine its strength and immune system.
>
> *(Krekó et al. 2019)*

Orbán sees Hungary as the great protector of Christian Europe, preserving it from these two corrupting influences.

The Hungarian churches echoed this stance from their government. A deputy bishop of the Reformed church said, "the uncontrolled admission of the flow of migrants from a different culture endangers European identity" (Kóczián 2022: 561). The Catholic bishops likewise called to "defend Christian Europe from the Muslim invasion." This is particularly striking in light of Pope Francis' pro-refugee stance and led to heightened tensions between the Hungarian bishops and the Vatican (Thorpe 2019: 33).

The official stance did not, of course, represent every Christian in Hungary. Many churches and charities responded with practical compassion and support for the incoming refugees, providing food, water, toilets, bedding, and help in reunifying separated families. Some Catholic priests and monks even opened their homes to asylum seekers, seeking to overturn Hungary's "reputation as haters of refugees" (Thorpe 2019: 238). The president of the European Commission pointed to "those Hungarian volunteers who give food and toys to hungry, exhausted refugee children" as the ones who represent the "real Europe" (Thorpe 2019: 75). Nevertheless, the majority aligned with the call for border closure of their ecclesial and political leaders.

One particular incident illustrates the cooperation between church and state on this issue. In 2016, the Hungarian government announced a national referendum on the following question: "Do you want the European Union to be able to mandate the obligatory resettlement of non-Hungarian citizens into Hungary even without the approval of the National Assembly?" (Thorpe 2019: 220). This was a shamelessly leading question framed to incline voters toward the government's preferred answer. There was almost no chance that the majority would vote "yes." Those in favor of refugee welcome began campaigning for people not to participate in the referendum because if voter turnout was below 50%, the referendum would be rendered invalid. But the Reformed Church urged everyone to vote, saying that the referendum concerned "the future of your children and grandchildren, the fate of your country, and Christian values" (Kóczián 2022: 562). This encouragement can only be interpreted as an anti-immigration move. This is all the more significant as it was the only official statement on immigration made by the Hungarian Reformed church throughout the period of the Syrian refugee crisis.

Such a hostility toward immigrants was not always the case in the Hungarian church. Thirty years earlier, it had enthusiastically supported immigrants and immigration. In the 1980s, a wave of refugees entered Hungary from Romania, fleeing dictatorial restrictions on their freedom. These were welcomed with open arms by the churches. The Reformed Church formally called for everyone to support the refugees, writing that "it is our Christian and national duty to provide everything we can to those who knock on the doors of our churches and congregations and ask for our help" (Kóczián 2022: 557). Here, we see a use of the word "Christian" that draws on religion's second meaning: ethical commitments. This throws into sharp relief the absence of this second meaning of religion – or more precisely, the absence of interest in what Christianity's ethical commitments might be – that we see in both Hungary's government and its official church position in 2015/2016.

Nor was anti-immigrant hostility always the case in Hungarian politics. Fidesz's appeal to preserve "traditional Hungarian values" appears unaware of the welcoming posture toward immigrants endorsed by one of its most celebrated heroes: King Saint Stephen of Hungary. The government holds up this eleventh-century monarch as Hungary's founding father. The "Fundamental Law of Hungary," written in 2011, contains the following proclamation in its preamble: "We are proud that our king Saint Stephen built the Hungarian State on solid ground and made our country a part of Christian Europe one thousand years ago" (Anon 2020). But this Catholic saint's immigration policy was the opposite of Fidesz's. One of his earliest hagiographies states that he "wanted his kingdom to be a refuge open to all foreigners" (Hartvic 2001: 390). In his instructions to his successor, he said that

> a country unified in language and in customs is fragile and weak. Therefore I order there, my son, to receive [all foreigners] with good will and to nourish them honestly in order that they abide with thee more joyfully than elsewhere.
> *(cited in Jászi 1929: 39)*

Again, we find the paradox that runs throughout this book: restricting immigration to preserve traditional Christian (even Hungarian in this case) values undermines those very values.

Indeed, a larger point could be made about the Hungarian government's use of the term "Christian/European values." Orbán, and Hungary following him, treats Christianity according to religion's first meaning alone: as a communal identity without reference to its beliefs or practices. What is noteworthy about all this talk of restricting immigration to preserve "Christian values" or "Christian identity" is that it makes no reference to *what* those Christian values are or *what* Christian identity comprises. They treat Christianity as an abstraction, a fungible "culture" to be preserved by whatever means necessary. Whether the means used to preserve the culture might conflict with that culture's own values or identity appears to be irrelevant.

What Orbán shows us is a picture of what Christianity looks like when it is treated solely as a communal identity and not as a set of beliefs and practices. He also shows us what happens when that communal identity is entangled with a nation-state. Without a doubt, Orbán has "combin[ed] national identity with religion" (Ewing 2017: 122). In fact, Christianity already has a community, called the Church, which since its inception has never been exclusively identified with a single nation-state. To be sure, the church has its own values, which it seeks to preserve. It does this by restricting church membership to those who sign up to Christian beliefs and commit to Christian practices. But Orbán has taken these legitimate boundary markers for church belonging and made them into entry requirements for *national citizenship*.

Angela Merkel and Germany

In both Hungary and Germany, the Syrian refugee crisis led to an appeal to "European values," but with strikingly different meanings. While Hungarian officials had talked *about* Christian or European values without mentioning *what* those values actually are, in Germany, the values themselves were invoked as reasons to welcome immigrants – values of compassion for the stranger, welcome of the "other," and support for the disadvantaged.

"The values of European civilization are at stake. . . . A Europe surrounded by fences will not work" (cited in Thorpe 2019: 64). Thus spoke the head of a German refugee charity defending Angela Merkel's decision to open Germany's borders. Similarly, the secretary-general of the Social Democratic Party claimed that Merkel's actions show how "European values are also valid in difficult times" (cited in Thorpe 2019: 97). Merkel herself referred to the need to uphold the "Universal civil rights" of the refugees as "essential European values" (Press Office 2015).

It is well known that Merkel did not consult her colleagues before making the decision to suspend the Dublin III regulations and open Germany's borders. This unilateral fiat needs to be explained first of all with reference to Merkel's motivations and character as an individual. Yet, at the same time, her action was not opposed to the values and principles of the people who elected her, as we shall see. We shall begin with a look at Merkel herself before seeing how her actions represented Germany as a whole.

Angela Merkel is a committed practicing Christian. In a 2012 interview, she said, "I am a member of the evangelical church. I believe in God and religion is also my constant companion, and has been for the whole of my life" (Spencer 2016). Unlike Orbán, who converted as an adult, Merkel was raised Christian, the daughter of a Lutheran pastor. When she was 6 weeks old, her father moved from West to East Germany due to a sense of calling to minister there, knowing it was a religiously challenging situation. The move came with many sacrifices. For example, Merkel's mother was a trained English teacher but was never allowed to teach for fear of the religious influence she might have on her pupils (Piel 2010).

Care for the marginalized and disadvantaged was part of Merkel's daily experience as a child. Another GDR pastor who knew her family reports that

> Her childhood home was not a normal Protestant parsonage, rather it was a church-run home for people with disabilities. Angela Kasner [her maiden name] grew up surrounded by disabled people who needed to be cared for. . . . Every day, Jesus and God were discussed in the Kasner household. . . . The daily message was: "Love thy neighbor as yourself. Not just German people. God loves everybody."
> *(Feldenkirchen & Pfister 2016)*

Mayer writes that "Merkel's leadership and political career are strongly influenced by her Christian values, her belief in God, and her Protestant religion" (Mayer 2021). Yet Merkel never liked to flaunt her faith. Most of the time, she kept it understated and private. When Barack Obama visited Germany, they prayed together in a church. But she did not let anyone photograph them, knowing that largely secular German society might react negatively to the image (Warner 2012).

Similarly, when explaining why she opened Germany's borders, she consistently gave rational and political justifications without any recourse to religion as a motivation. She said, for example, that if she closed the borders, the refugees would pile up in the fragile Balkan states and risk destabilizing them. Yet these justifications do not tell the whole story since they would have applied equally well to Hungary. They do not account for her stubborn refusal to put a cap on immigrant numbers in spite of mounting criticism both inside and outside her party or for the dramatic decline in her popularity as a consequence of her decision. It was also uncharacteristic of her to be so uncompromising, as she had hitherto been known as a pragmatic figure without a strong political agenda.

However, despite the uniqueness of her stance, it was not unrepresentative of the German people. When the strategic justifications became unsupportable, she appealed instead to German values and to her place within them:

> To the criticism that Germany is allowing in too many refugees, [Merkel responded:] "If we now have to start apologizing for showing a friendly face in response to emergency situations, then that's not my country." . . . It wasn't a political tactician speaking this time, but a compassionate pastor's daughter from the eastern state of Brandenburg – a politician who remains acutely aware of the Christian element in her party's agenda.
>
> *(Nelles 2015)*

This quote shows the connection between Merkel's personal faith and the way she appeals to traditional German identity. The two are not opposed but come from the same source: Christianity. Merkel was simply acting on behalf of Germany's better nature, the nature formed by centuries of Christian principles, a nature that Germany sometimes forgot but had never completely lost. "Our society lives on premises that it cannot create by itself," she said in 2010:

> Without a doubt, one of these very important premises is Christianity. . . . That means we know that freedom does not mean freedom from something, but it means freedom given by God through His Creation to commit oneself to help others and stand up for causes.
>
> *(cited in Spencer 2017: 163)*

Seven years later, she felt the same way:

> It feels to me that we live always on the basis of premises that we cannot create, but are rooted in our history, in our

convictions and our faith. These premises carry us into the
future and lead us a little out of our self-centeredness.
(Merkel 2017: 31–2)

For Merkel, these three things are the same: (1) the foundations of German society, (2) Christian values, and (3) "helping others" due to having been led "out of our self-centeredness."

The German churches quickly rallied in support of her decision. The heads of both the German Catholic and the national Protestant churches went with her to the train station at Munich to greet the first trainload of refugees. Both also issued public statements calling for all of Germany to adopt a "culture of mercy, humanity, acceptance, open-mindedness, and diversity" (Mielke 2016).

"It would be naïve," writes Spencer, "to trace [Merkel's position on immigration] back to the Old Testament legislation on the imperative of hospitality to the stranger" (Spencer 2016). No Christian, no matter how integralist, wants to copy–paste Israelite law onto the contemporary political scene. Yet the values contained in the Christian tradition, values that once manifested in the Israelite care for strangers, may manifest in the same way and for the same reason today through people who have steeped themselves in those values through lifelong formation in Christian virtue. In a speech in 2017, she said the following:

> I believe religious education is increasingly more, not less important in our time, because it is about the formation of heart and conscience, and because it is about more than just our own life, but it is about the great interrelatedness of our lives as God's creatures. . . . All of us live from premises that we cannot create, but are grounded in our history, our convictions, and our faith, and which carry us into the future and lead us step by step out of our self-centeredness.
> *(Merkel 2017: 31)*

Merkel explicitly connects Christian formation with her chosen response to refugees. For her, enacting Christian values is not a matter of legalistic obedience to proof texts plucked from the

Bible, however applicable such texts might be. Rather, it is about the lifelong cultivation of Christian character that becomes second nature so that all our decisions and actions arise instinctively from virtues instilled by Christian education. Religious practice cultivates an instinct for the good because it is a meditation on the source of all good and the purpose of our existence. We act in a Christian way even when we cannot point to a theological argument to justify it because we have been steeped in Christian ways of thinking. Merkel not only understands this, but also she herself is a clear example of political action motivated by subterranean Christian ideals.

Conclusion

Orbán and Merkel responded in opposite ways to the Syrian refugee crisis, yet both the anti-immigrant and pro-immigrant stances arose from their Christian convictions and identities. To call the responses "religiously motivated" does not mean that religion was their sole and sufficient *cause*. Religious motivation does not need to be separate from economic, political, or other motivations in order to be real. Human beings typically have multiple motivations for any action and can truthfully point to any of them as a reason. What this chapter has shown is that religion, both as common identity and as ethical commitments, lies behind much of the activity of the 2015 Syrian refugee crisis.

The events reveal a paradox at the heart of Christian immigration ethics. Christianity means membership in a community with a shared set of beliefs, values, and ways of life. One of those Christian values is welcoming the "other," even if that "other" does not share those beliefs, values, and ways of life. On the one hand, to refuse the welcome of the other is to betray Christian values and cease to be Christian (except in name). On the other hand, to welcome a great many "others" with different values means that Christian values are no longer normative in the public square and that the national community loses its Christian self-understanding. A despairing outlook might say that Christianity is doomed: either it undermines its own values in its struggle to preserve itself, or it sits by to watch those values be swept away by mass immigration. A more optimistic outlook might point to a mysterious saying of Jesus that suggests a solution to the paradox: "those who want to save their life will lose it, and those who lose their life for my sake will find it" (Matt 16:25 NRSV). Perhaps self-defense, self-preservation, and self-protection are not the Christian way; rather, an open and self-sacrificial welcome that does not fear the erosion of Christian values is in fact at the very core of the way of being that Jesus taught and exemplified. As Merkel said in response to the worry that Islam will transform German culture: "we don't have too much Islam, we have too little Christianity, we have too few discussions about the Christian view of mankind" (The Economist 2016).

References

Ádám, Zoltán, and András Bozóki. (2016). "State and Faith: Right-Wing Populism and Nationalized Religion in Hungary". *Intersections: East European Journal of Society and Politics* 2(1).

Anon. (2020). "The Fundamental Law of Hungary". Viewed from: https://www.parlament.hu/documents/125505/138409/Fundamental+law/73811993-c377-428d-9808-ee03d6fb8178 [Date accessed: 14 July 2025].

Bauman, Stephan, Matthew Soerens, and Dr. Issam Smeir. (2016). *Seeking Refuge: On the Shores of the Global Refugee Crisis*. Moody Publishers.

Bender, Felix. (2020). "Abolishing Asylum and Violating the Human Rights of Refugees: Why Is It Tolerated?: The Case of Hungary in the EU". Pp. 59–73 in *Europe and the Refugee Response: A Crisis of Values?*, Routledge Studies in Development, Displacement and Resettlement, edited by E. M. Goździak, I. Main, and B. Suter. New York: Routledge.

Betts, Alexander, and Paul Collier. (2018). *Refuge: Transforming a Broken Refugee System*. London: Penguin.

The Economist. (2016). "German Politicians Are Both More and Less Religious Than British Ones". *The Economist*, January 7. Viewed from: www.economist.com/erasmus/2016/01/07/german-politicians-are-both-more-and-less-religious-than-british-ones [Date accessed: 24 June 2024].

Ewing, Joseph. (2017). "Viktor Orbán". in *The Mighty and the Almighty: How Political Leaders Do God*, edited by N. Spencer. London: Biteback Publishing.

Faiola, Anthony, and Michael Birnbaum. (2015). "Pope Calls on Europe's Catholics to Take in Refugees". *The Washington Post*, September 6. Viewed from: www.washingtonpost.com/world/refugees-keep-streaming-into-europe-as-crisis-continues-unabated/2015/09/06/8a330572-5345-11e5-b225-90edbd49f362_story.html [Date accessed: 26 March 2025].

Feldenkirchen, Markus, and René Pfister. (2016). "Why Has Angela Merkel Staked Her Legacy on the Refugees?" *Der Spiegel*, January 25. Viewed from: www.spiegel.de/international/germany/why-has-angela-merkel-staked-her-legacy-on-the-refugees-a-1073705.html [Date accessed: 7 June 2024].

Gallaher, Carolyn, and Garret Martin. (2020). "Viktor Orbán's Use and Misuse of Religion Serves as a Warning to Western Democracies". *The Conversation*, October 27. Viewed from: http://theconversation.com/viktor-orbans-use-and-misuse-of-religion-serves-as-a-warning-to-western-democracies-146277 [Date accessed: 12 June 2024].

Hartvic. (2001). "Life of King Stephen of Hungary". in *Medieval Hagiography: An Anthology*. Psychology Press.

Jászi, Oscar. (1929). *The Dissolution of the Habsburg Monarchy*. University of Chicago Press.

Kepplinger, H. M. (2019). "Die Mediatisierung der Migrationspolitik und Angela Merkels Entschei-dungspraxis". Pp. 195–217 in *Zwischen Stillstand, Politikwandel und Krisenmanagement. Eine Bilanz der Regierung Merkel 2013–2017*, edited by R. Zohlnhöfer and T. Saalfeld. Wiesbaden: Springer.

Kóczián, Viktória. (2022). "'This Nest Is for All Kinds of Birds'? National Identity Questions in the Refugee Reception of the Reformed Church in Hungary". *Religion, State and Society* 50(5): 553–68.

Krekó, Péter, Bulcsú Hunyadi, and Patrik Szicherle. (2019). *Anti-Muslim Populism in Hungary: From the Margins to the Mainstream*. Brookings Institution.

Lendvai, Paul. (2018). *Orbán: Hungary's Strongman*. Oxford University Press.

Mayer, Claude-Hélène. (2021). "Leading with Faith: Angela Merkel in Psychobiographical Perspective". Pp. 32–46 in *Reimagining Faith and Management*, edited by E. Pio, T. Pratt, and R. Kilpatrick. Abingdon: Routledge.

Merkel, Angela. (2017). *Daran Glaube Ich: Christliche Standpunkte*. Edited by V. Resing. Leipzig: Benno Verlag.

Meszaros, Edina Lilla. (2019). "The Politicization, Mediatisation and the Visual Framing of the Refugee Crisis in Hungary". in

Muslim Minorities and the Refugee Crisis in Europe, edited by K. Górak-Sosnowska, M. Pachocka, and J. Misiuna. Warsaw: SGH Publishing House.

Mielke, Roger. (2016). 'Stewarding Mercy'. *Plough*, December 16. Viewed from: www.plough.com/en/topics/justice/social-justice/immigration/stewarding-mercy [Date accessed: 24 June 2024].

Morina, Drenusha. (2024). "Number of Immigrants in Hungary Saw a Notable Surge, Reaching over 403,000 in 2023". *Schengen News*, June 12. Viewed from: https://schengen.news/number-of-immigrants-in-hungary-saw-a-notable-surge-reaching-over-403000-in-2023/ [Date accessed: 3 July 2024].

Müller-Brandeck-Bocquet, Gisela. (2022). "Angela Merkel and the Refugee Crisis of 2015: Events, Decisions and Consequences". Pp. 61–79 in *Germany and the European Union: How Chancellor Angela Merkel Shaped Europe*. Cham: Springer International Publishing.

Nelles, Roland. (2015). "Merkel Refuses to Apologize for Welcoming Refugees". *Der Spiegel*, September 16. Viewed from: www.spiegel.de/international/germany/merkel-refuses-to-apologize-for-welcoming-refugees-a-1053253.html [Date accessed: 21 June 2024].

Piel, Monika. (2010). "Tel est mon destin: Entretien avec Angela Merkel". *Politique Internationale*. Viewed from: https://politiqueinternationale.com/revue/n127/article/tel-est-mon-destin [Date accessed: 24 June 2024].

Press Office. (2015). "Flexibility Is Called for Now". *The Press and Information Office of the Federal Government*, August 31. Viewed from: www.bundesregierung.de/breg-en/service/archive/archive/-flexibility-is-called-for-now–435220 [Date accessed: 21 June 2024].

Schmiedel, Ulrich, and Graeme Smith. (2018). "Introduction: Charting a Crisis". in *Religion in the European Refugee Crisis, Religion and Global Migrations*, edited by G. Smith and U. Schmiedel. Cham: Palgrave Macmillan.

Spencer, Nick. (2016). "Merkel's Strong, Unshowy Faith". *Church Times*, February 26. Viewed from: www.churchtimes.co.uk/articles/2016/26-february/comment/columnists/merkel-s-strong-unshowy-faith [Date accessed: 21 June 2024].

Spencer, Nick. (2017). "Angela Merkel". in *The Mighty and the Almighty: How Political Leaders Do God*, edited by N. Spencer. London: Biteback Publishing.

Thorpe, Nick. (2019). *The Road before Me Weeps: On the Refugee Route through Europe*. New Haven: Yale University Press.

Traynor, Ian. (2015). "Migration Crisis: Hungary PM Says Europe in Grip of Madness". *The Guardian*, September 3. Viewed from: www.theguardian.com/world/2015/sep/03/migration-crisis-hungary-pm-victor-orban-europe-response-madness [Date accessed: 12 June 2024].

Warner, Mary Beth. (2012). "Merkel Raises Eyebrows by Raising Religion". *Global Post*, November 27. Viewed from: https://theworld.org/stories/2016/07/31/merkel-raises-eyebrows-raising-religion [Date accessed: 21 June 2024].

World Council of Churches, Conference of European Churches, and Churches' Commission for Migrants in Europe. (2015). "European Refugee Situation: Churches' Initiatives for Refugees and Other Migrants". Viewed from: www.oikoumene.org/sites/default/files/Document/Letter%20on%20European%20refugee%20situation.pdf. [Date accessed: 26 March 2025].

NOW WHAT? IMPLICATIONS FOR ACADEMICS, POLICYMAKERS, AND PRACTITIONERS

If there is any question about whether conflicts over immigration policy will be with us for the foreseeable future, recent events that fill pages of newspapers and hours of media coverage make clear policy debates will only increase. In Germany, when the CDU leader Friedrich Merz proposed an anti-immigrant policy that depended on AfD support, even former Chancellor Angela Merkel protested, opening a breach in the party.

All around the world, religion is the fuel that ignites anti-immigrant violence and assaults on those not deemed authentic citizens. At the same time, religious leaders are often the ones protesting anti-immigrant policies, calling for compassion and support for those fleeing violence and poverty. Policymakers will need to deal not only with the pragmatic questions that surround immigration, such as housing and border controls, opportunities for work, and eventual citizenship, but also with how to integrate these policies with competing religious demands for and against immigration. The urgency and importance of rightly understanding the relationship between religion and immigration have been demonstrated throughout this book, but we will offer one final illustration here because, although it does not fit in the above chapters or case studies, its relevance serves as a striking example of all that this book is about.

A Vignette: Pope Francis, J.D. Vance, and the *Ordo Amoris*

Donald Trump's successful campaign for reelection as president led to large-scale actions in 2025 to deport undocumented immigrants, cut funding for refugee charities, suspend refugee admissions, and revoke the legal status of some categories of immigrants who entered legally under the Biden administration (Brennan 2025; Hesson & Cooke 2025; Montoya-Galvez 2025). In defense of these actions, US Vice President J.D. Vance turned to the fifth "basic Christian principle" we outlined in Chapter 2 of this book. In a TV interview, Vance said that it was a

> Christian concept . . . that you love your family, and then you love your neighbor, and then you love your community, and then you love your fellow citizens in your own country, and then, after that, you can focus and prioritize the rest of the world.
>
> *(Fox News 2025)*

When this viewpoint was criticized on X by former British MP Rory Stewart, an Anglican, Vance replied, "Just google 'ordo amoris'," a tweet that received over 11 million views (Vance 2025).

As the debate escalated, it drew attention from scholars and politicians across the globe. Dr. James Orr, Associate Professor of Philosophy of Religion at the University of Cambridge, defended Vance's position as "stating the obvious" with regard to Christian values and said that "the man who, when faced with the choice of saving his drowning wife or a drowning stranger, hesitates to consider which course of action would contribute more to the overall good of humanity has had one thought too many" (Orr 2025). Taking a different stance, Frederick Bauerschmidt, Professor of Theology at Loyola University Maryland, and Maureen Sweeney, an expert in immigration law, pointed to Aquinas' careful and nuanced formulation of the principle (discussed in Chapter 2 of this book) to conclude that "the *ordo amoris* may not require us to treat these strangers as if they were our own children, but it also does not give us *carte blanche* to put off addressing their urgent human need" (Bauerschmidt & Sweeney 2025). Graham Tomlin, an Anglican bishop based in London, pointed out that, for the progenitors of the *ordo amoris* such as Augustine and Aquinas, love is not a finite resource like cake with a limited number of slices but is better compared to fire:

> When you take a light from a candle and light another candle with it, the first candle is not diminished, but continues to burn brightly. Fire can be passed on from one place to another and spread widely because it's not finite in the way that a cake is. . . . Loving our family and friends is therefore a kind of tutorial in divine love, the kind that spreads like fire. Practicing the art of love on those closest to us helps us learn the skills of loving others. Loving my family teaches me to love my friends. Loving my friends teaches me to love my neighbors. Loving my neighbors teaches me how to love the stranger.
> *(Tomlin 2025)*

Even Pope Francis weighed in with a letter to the US Catholic Bishops, writing that

> the true *ordo amoris* that must be promoted is that which we discover by meditating constantly on the parable of the "Good Samaritan" (cf. *Lk* 10:25–37), that is, by meditating on the love that builds a fraternity open to all, without exception.
> *(Pope Francis 2025)*

It would not be accurate to say that Vance is ignorant of the Christian tradition since he knew enough to invoke the ancient principle using its Latin term. But, as we saw in Chapter 2, the *ordo amoris* contains nuanced advice about how to weigh proximity against need. Aquinas wrote that "in certain cases one ought, for instance, to succor a stranger, in extreme necessity, rather than one's own father, if he is not in such urgent need" (Aquinas 1911: *Summa Theologiae* II-II.Q31.A3.C). This aspect did not appear in any of the articles and blog posts defending Vance's position, yet it would be known to anyone who has steeped themselves in the Catholic tradition and who sought to understand the *ordo amoris* in all its depth so as to live by it. Once again, we find an anti-immigrant sentiment arising from those who draw a connection between national identity and religious identity by means of the *ordo amoris* in this case, its goal being to justify the policy of "putting America first." And once again, we find that those who dig deeper into the tradition learn a different story, a reason to show solidarity with refugees and all those fleeing their homeland to escape desperate situations.

Final Recommendations

In light of these realities, our first recommendation to policymakers, academics, and practitioners is simply to understand the power of religion to motivate immigration policies across the political spectrum. In some ways, this seems counterintuitive, especially in nations that ostensibly separate church and state. But in the second decade of the twenty-first century, the resurgence of religion in partisan politics demands taking religious values and viewpoints very seriously. Since religious fervor is often at the core of mobilizing citizen groups and political movements, we strongly encourage political leaders and policymakers to proactively engage religious leaders when considering immigration policy, even grounding their decisions in values and language that speak to the religious faithful. Navigating immigration policy conflicts will need great skill and sensitivity, so awareness of how religion impacts the political environment is crucial. That means learning what, in particular, the dominant religion has to say and what counterviews are being offered, both from within the dominant religion and by minority faith communities. That is what we have illustrated in this book, modeling what policymakers and political leaders need to know about Christianity in Hungary and Germany and Judaism in Israel and the United States.

Second, we recommend a two-category heuristic tool for discerning the way religion is understood by its adherents. While numerous definitions of "religion" are available, and some by contrast deny any stable meaning to the word, we believe that when it comes to immigration policy, two stand out as the most useful: religion as communal/national identity and religion as beliefs and practices. These are not mutually exclusive: a person may understand their faith in both ways at once. But we have detected a broad trend, not without exceptions, that hostility toward immigrants arises more frequently from those who construe their religion in terms of communal/national identity, whereas welcoming of immigrants arises more frequently among those who spend more time in religious practice. Religious practice includes reflecting on the scriptural and traditional sources of moral guidance.

Third, we recommend that attention be paid to the instances where religious identity overlaps with national identity. In the contemporary period, those who seek such an overlap tend to appeal to the preservation of their culture's traditional values, which are often rooted in their religious heritage but not always in religious belief or practice. A religious community does not necessarily have territory or borders. Its membership can be voluntary and without any relationship to politics. The religious "other" can be loved, respected, and welcomed without compromising the group's identity. However, when religious identity overlaps with national identity, a complex tension is created in the maintenance of national borders. The welcome of strangers becomes perceived as a threat to the coherence of the nation, its cultural values, and its identity. Both Christianity and Judaism have adherents who see immigration as a malevolent threat to their national enterprise, a threat that undermines the nation.

Fourth and finally, we recommend that everyone, religious or otherwise, acquire a deeper familiarity with the sacred texts at the heart of Judaism, Christianity, and Islam. The scriptures of these faiths contain manifold injunctions to welcome and love strangers, not as an isolated exception but as an instance of a broader concern for the marginalized, disadvantaged, and poor. Yet texts can always be interpreted in more than one way, and interpretations are shaped by powerful interests and agendas. Religious texts can be a pretext for justifying policy, and, in most cases, alternative texts would support an opposite policy position. Nevertheless, many of the social science studies we have cited in this book show a tendency among the faithful who regularly read their scriptures (and engage in other forms of religious practice) to advocate more inclusive and welcoming immigration policies than those who identify with the religion at a nominal or cultural level. There are exceptions, even among religious leaders and scholars, and these are often the most vocal, but they do not nullify this trend.

Displacement caused by famine, climate change, war, and gang violence is not diminishing. The dream of the immigrant, to find a better life for oneself and one's family, will hardly weaken in spite of the intense opposition they may face. These realities only add to the challenges policymakers, political leaders, and voters face as they continue to navigate the demands that immigrants will make on the political, social, and economic structures of many nations. Elections will be determined by the ways political parties and their leaders respond to the competing demands of religion, knowing that religious communities play a significant role in mobilizing the faithful and often claim a powerful moral voice in so many nations, including those we have explored in our case studies. That is why it is essential for anyone concerned with immigration policy to understand the complicated ways Judaism and Christianity handle the topic. While we share a concern about the experiences and sufferings of immigrants, we have focused on policy and the attitudes of citizens toward immigrants in order to highlight the power of religion in international politics.

In particular, we share the concern that so many have over the violent rhetoric and, even more, the violent behavior that so often erupts when immigration policy is debated. The potential for polarizing civil conflict threatens politicians, immigrants, and citizens alike. The murder of pro-immigration Walter Lübcke in Germany by a far-right sympathizer and the riots and burnings in the United Kingdom, Germany, Los Angeles, and Myanmar in the past years remind us of the potential for violence that undermines democracy and threatens rational, thoughtful policymaking. Invoking religious values of compassion and love and calling on religious leaders to calm the anger are tools that political leaders could use when immigration conflict erupts.

Judeo-Christian values, to the extent that they exist beyond platitudes, are often seen as the bedrock that defines the modern Western world. They include kindness and respect for all people instead of power, humility instead of status, honesty and generosity instead of wealth, self-control instead of self-indulgence, and forgiveness instead of revenge while promoting peace and goodwill among people. Yet no community can allow for radical inclusiveness and maintain its shared unique solidarity. Whether formed through common beliefs, practices, ethnicity, dress, diet, or something else, a religion's identity depends on its members having something in common. There will always be an "other," someone who, if only by choice, does not share that identity.

As all the recent national elections in the West demonstrate, the question of who belongs, and who should have status as citizen, is a central issue to many voters. Among the more populist politicians and political parties, denouncing immigrants and calling for the expulsion of unwanted elements within the country as invasive threats are at the core of their rhetoric.

For leaders and followers, for the faithful who attend religious services regularly to hear Holy Scripture recited, and for those who never set foot in a religious setting yet see their identity tied to historic religious connections, it remains the case that the political and societal attitudes toward those not native-born are often expressed in terms of religious identity as well as religious values. The intersection of immigration policy and religion, more powerful than economic concerns, needs to be highlighted. It is to this end that we have written this volume.

References

Aquinas, St. Thomas. (1911). *Summa Theologiae*. New York: Benziger Bros.

Bauerschmidt, Frederick, and Maureen Sweeney. (2025). "Ordo Amoris: Wisely Extending Love". *Church Life Journal*, February 6. Viewed from: https://churchlifejournal.nd.edu/articles/ordo-amoris-wisely-extending-love/ [Date accessed: 25 March 2025].

Brennan, Margaret. (2025). "Transcript: Vice President JD Vance on 'Face the Nation with Margaret Brennan'". *CBS News*, January 26. Viewed from: www.cbsnews.com/news/jd-vance-transcript-face-the-nation-01-26-2025/ [Date accessed: 25 March 2025].

Fox News. (2025). "JD Vance: President Trump Is Looking after American Citizens". Viewed from: https://www.youtube.com/watch?v=o98Po0lWZxE [Date accessed: 14 July 2025].

Hesson, Ted, and Kristina Cooke. (2025). "Trump Weighs Revoking Legal Status of Ukrainians as US Steps up Deportations". *Reuters*, March 7. Viewed from: www.reuters.com/world/us/trump-plans-revoke-legal-status-ukrainians-who-fled-us-sources-say-2025-03-06/ [Date accessed: 25 March 2025].

Montoya-Galvez, Camilo. (2025). "U.S. to Revoke Legal Status of More Than a Half-Million Migrants, Urges Them to Self Deport – CBS News". *CBS News*, March 23. Viewed from: www.cbsnews.com/news/u-s-to-revoke-legal-status-of-over-a-half-million-migrants-chnv/ [Date accessed: 25 March 2025].

Orr, James. (2025). "JD Vance States the Obvious about Ordo Amoris". *First Things*, January 31. Viewed from: https://firstthings.com/jd-vance-states-the-obvious-about-ordo-amoris/ [Date accessed: 25 March 2025].

Pope Francis. (2025). "Letter of the Holy Father to the Bishops of the United States of America". Viewed from: https://www.vatican.va/content/francesco/en/letters/2025/documents/20250210-lettera-vescovi-usa.html [Date accessed: 25 March 2025].

Tomlin, Graham. (2025). "JD Vance and Rory Stewart Have Both Missed the Point When It Comes to Who to Love". *Seen & Unseen*, February 3. Viewed from: www.seenandunseen.com/jd-vance-and-rory-stewart-have-both-missed-point-when-it-comes-who-love [Date accessed: 25 March 2025].

Vance, J. D. (2025). "Just Google 'Ordo Amoris': Aside from That, the Idea That There Isn't a Hierarchy of Obligations Violates Basic Common Sense. Does Rory Really Think His Moral Duties to His Own Children Are the Same as His Duties to a Stranger Who Lives Thousands of Miles Away? Does Anyone?" *Twitter*. Viewed from: https://x.com/JDVance/status/1885073046400012538 [Date accessed: 25 March 2025].

INDEX

abortion 84
Abraham 16, 17, 57, 94
accompaniment 51
Adam 57
Afghanistan 53, 92
Africa 79, 82, 88
Agnosticism 4
Aleinikoff, Alexander 2, 12
America 5, 10–12, 23, 24, 26–28, 31, 54–56, 59, 61, 77, 78, 84–87, 113
Anabaptist 59
Anglicanism 40, 41, 111, 112
anti-immigration 7, 12, 32, 37, 39, 42, 43, 49, 52, 56, 67, 83, 87, 99, 105, 110, 113
Antisemitism 44, 45
apartheid 65
Appiah, Kwame 2, 12
Aquinas 34, 68, 111, 112, 116
Arab 6, 83
Aristotle 37
asylum 6, 27, 28, 39, 41, 51, 79, 82, 83, 87, 88, 92, 93, 98, 106
atheist 4, 40, 78

Baggio, Fabio 50
Balog, Zoltan 96

Bauerschmidt, Frederick 111, 112, 116
Betts, Alexander 94, 106
Bible, biblical 9, 10, 14–20, 23, 27, 31, 33, 41, 42, 47, 54, 56–68, 79, 81, 85, 86, 105
Biden, Joe 111
blasphemy 9, 17, 18, 22
borders 14, 32, 35, 50, 58, 62–64, 67, 91–93, 97, 98, 101, 102, 110, 114
boundary 6, 17, 62, 63, 101
Buddhist 6, 9

Canaanite 14, 17
Carroll, Daniel 61
Catholicism 10–12, 31, 36–39, 41–44, 49–55, 68, 93, 95, 96, 98, 100, 104, 112
Cavanaugh, William 3, 12
Charlie Hebdo 94
Christendom 42, 44
Christianity 5, 9, 10, 12, 19, 22, 23, 31–33, 35–37, 39–49, 53–63, 65–67, 85, 91, 94–106, 111–115
church 5, 12, 31, 33, 35–37, 39–45, 49, 50, 52–54, 56,

57, 59, 68, 93, 96, 98–102, 104, 113
church of England *see* Anglicanism
citizen 5, 7–9, 11, 14, 18, 19, 24–28, 33, 34, 36, 54, 60, 61, 63–65, 67, 78, 80, 92, 99, 101, 110, 111, 113, 115, 116
civilization 44, 101
climate 1, 12, 26, 115
coercion 47
coexistence 83
colonialism 58
community 3–7, 9, 10, 16, 17, 19, 20, 24–27, 31, 40, 42, 45–47, 50, 52, 58, 77, 78, 81, 86, 87, 91, 93, 94, 97, 100, 105, 111, 113–116
compassion 2, 11, 21, 33, 38, 41, 50, 59, 86, 88, 93, 94, 98, 101, 103, 110, 115
cosmopolitanism 62
Cremer, Tobias 42–44, 55, 56
Czech Republic 36, 38, 39

D'Costa, Gavin 49
Dawkins, Richard 40
dehumanizing 53
democracy 23, 24, 51, 80, 96, 101, 115
deport, deportation 12, 41, 42, 82, 88, 111
Deuteronomy 14, 18, 20, 60, 62
diaspora 10, 15, 16, 24–28, 77, 84, 86
disability 33, 102
Drollinger, Ralph 61, 62, 64, 65
Dublin Regulation 92, 93, 101

economics 2, 9, 26, 45, 46, 51, 78, 92, 94, 95, 105, 115, 116

Egypt 14, 15, 18, 19, 21, 28, 50, 57, 60, 66, 81, 86
Elijah 57
England *see* United Kingdom
Enlightenment 24
erga migrantes caritas 50, 51
Ethiopia 81
ethnicity 5, 7, 16, 23, 26, 32–34, 36, 38, 77, 80, 84, 116
Europe 5, 10–12, 19, 24, 27, 31, 32, 35, 36, 40–46, 49, 56, 79, 85, 86, 91–94, 97, 98, 100, 101, 106
European Union 12, 98
Evangelicalism 10, 23, 31, 54–57, 67, 101
evangelism 45, 47
exile 17, 50, 57, 77, 78, 85
expulsion 6, 9, 17, 23, 45–49, 68, 79, 82, 83, 116
extremism 23, 59, 91

faith 2, 5, 6, 9–11, 17, 20, 24, 26, 31, 32, 38–40, 42–44, 52–56, 68, 88, 94, 96, 102–104, 106, 113–116
far-right 42, 43, 115
Fidesz 95–100
Filipino 36
forced migration 1, 33, 50, 53
foreign 2, 7, 10, 12, 16–18, 31, 34, 52, 60, 61, 79, 81–83, 95, 100
forgiveness 116
fratelli tutti 50, 52
fundamentalism 23

Galli, Mark 56
Gaza 18, 82
genocide 17, 27
gentile 19–22, 47, 81, 85
Germany 9, 10, 12, 35, 41–43, 45, 91, 93–95, 101–104, 110, 113, 115

ghetto 45, 46, 48
Gibney, Matthew 62
Glanville, Mark & Luke 61, 63, 65, 66
Gospel, the 39, 48
government 11, 23, 27, 33, 35–37, 39–42, 51, 58, 59, 61–65, 67, 78–80, 82, 83, 88, 92, 95, 98–100
grace 86
Greece 37, 92

Hafetz Hayyim 25
Haggadah 28
Hagiography 100
Haidt, Jonathan 17
halakhic 25, 77
Hamas 82
Hebraeorum Gens 48
Hebrew 6, 26, 58–60, 66
Heimburger, Robert 63
Hinduism 6, 9
Hoffmeier, James 61, 64, 66, 67
Hollenbach, David 32
Holocaust 15, 26, 28, 78
home 1, 2, 16, 23, 24, 26, 37, 40, 41, 51, 61, 79, 92, 93, 98, 102, 113
hospitality 8, 25, 39, 104
hostile 2, 6, 8, 10, 31, 36, 40, 41, 43, 44, 49, 99, 114
Hungary 9, 10, 35, 85, 91–102, 106, 113

identity 2–9, 11, 12, 15–17, 19, 22, 24, 26, 28, 31, 32, 36–40, 42–44, 49, 52, 59, 65–68, 77, 79–81, 84, 88, 91, 94, 97, 98, 100, 103, 105, 113–116
ideology 12, 18, 58, 98
illegal immigration 37, 41, 65
imago Dei 32, 33

immigrant 2, 7, 8, 10, 12, 15, 26, 28, 35–42, 50, 52, 56, 61, 63, 65–67, 79, 80, 83, 84, 86–88, 95, 99, 101, 102, 111, 114–116
immigration 1–12, 14, 15, 26–28, 31, 32, 35, 36, 41, 43–45, 49–51, 53–58, 60, 61, 63–67, 77, 78, 80, 81, 83–88, 92, 95, 97, 99, 100, 104–106, 110, 111, 113–116
inclusivity 5, 6, 10, 20, 78, 81, 115, 116
India 1, 4, 6, 9, 81
Indonesia 4, 9
Injustice 39
integration 2, 24, 26, 36, 50, 60, 93, 110
invasion 9, 41, 97, 98, 116
Islam 9, 10, 35, 37, 40–44, 98, 106, 114
Islamophobia 37
Israel 1, 4, 6, 9, 10, 14–23, 25–27, 57, 58, 60, 61, 63, 77–84, 88, 104, 113
Italy 11, 41, 42, 47

Jesus 39, 47–50, 57–59, 64–67, 102, 106
Jews 5, 6, 9, 10, 14–16, 18–28, 44–49, 55, 68, 77–88
John Paul II 50, 51
Judaism 9, 10, 14–16, 20, 23, 24, 26, 27, 46, 47, 58, 77, 81, 113–115
Judaizers 46, 47
Judeo-Christian 115

Kamen, Henry 46

laicité 6
Le Pen, Jean-Marie 43

left-wing 55
Leuștean, Lucian 7, 53, 54
libertarianism 59
Locke, John 59
Lutheranism 39, 102

Magisterium, Catholic 49
Merkel, Angela 11, 91, 93–95, 101–106, 110
migrant 6, 11, 33, 35, 39, 42, 43, 50–54, 57, 82, 91–94, 97, 98
migration 1, 7, 11, 12, 16, 20, 40, 41, 44, 49–53, 57
Mishnah 19–21, 25, 78
mitzvah 22, 77, 78
modernity 24, 32
Muslim 5, 6, 9, 22, 35–38, 43, 68, 79, 81, 91, 94, 95, 97, 98
Myanmar 4, 6, 9, 115

nationalism, nationalist 4, 39, 41, 52–54, 59, 82
nation-state 1, 7, 26, 44, 50, 58, 100
naturalization 18
Netanyahu, Bibi 82
Nigeria 4

Obama, Barack 102
oppression 15, 16, 21, 27, 28, 33, 60, 68, 77, 86, 91
Orbán, Viktor 91–98, 100, 101, 105, 106
ordo amoris 33, 35, 111–113, 116
ordo amoris 33, 35, 111–113, 116
Orthodox Church, The 31, 53, 54
Orthodox Judaism 22, 80, 81, 86

ostracization 2
othering 15

Palestine 18, 23, 24, 78, 79, 81–83
Papacy 11, 37, 43, 45, 47–52, 93, 98, 111, 112
PEGIDA 42
Peppiatt, Lucy 32
Philippines 36
Poland 4, 36–39, 68
pope *see* Papacy
Pope Francis 11, 37, 52, 93, 98, 111, 112
Pope John Paul II 50, 51
Pope Paul IV 45
Pope Pius V 45, 48, 49
Pope Pius XII 50
populism 35, 42, 52, 53, 56, 57, 83, 106, 116
prayer 2, 41, 82, 88, 96, 102
pro-immigration 7, 42, 52, 55, 56, 68, 87, 98, 105, 115
Protestantism 12, 55, 102, 104
Purim 81
Putin, Vladimir 9

rabbinic 15, 19–21, 25–27, 79, 84
racism 23, 36, 52
Ramadan 40
Rassemblement National (French political party) 43
refugee 1, 6, 11, 12, 15, 26–28, 35–40, 42, 43, 50, 51, 54, 59, 66, 67, 77, 79, 82–84, 86–88, 91–95, 97–99, 101–106, 111, 113
Republican Party, US 55
residency, permanent 95
right-wing 42, 53, 55, 56, 80, 82, 106
ritual 5, 16, 36, 61, 78, 84, 86

Rohingya Muslims 9
Romania 99
Rowley, Matthew 8
Russia 9, 54
Rwanda 41, 82

Sabbath 25, 80, 81
Schengen Area 92, 93, 95
Schmiedel, Ulrich 92
secularization 4, 5, 12, 19, 39, 43, 44, 49, 95–97, 102
Serbia 92
slavery 48, 57, 61
social justice 2, 26, 27, 91
Soerens, Matthew 65, 106
solidarity 2, 33, 51, 52, 91, 113, 116
Soviet Union 80, 96
Spain 19, 45–48
Stackhouse, John 57
synagogue 26, 27, 86, 88
synod 54

table 46
tacitly 87
takes 8, 10, 25, 50, 81
talisman 2
talk 40, 96, 100
Talmud 20, 27
Tanya 21, 22
task 58
teach 42, 102
teachers 53
teaches 32, 33, 68, 112
tears 21
tend 31, 32, 39, 41, 42, 53, 56, 67, 114
tension 5, 10, 15, 25, 50, 114
terms 12, 38, 41, 114, 116
territorial 62
terrorist 37
testify 48
testimony 88

texts 6, 10, 16, 22, 27, 28, 46, 51, 58, 67, 77, 78, 82, 84–86, 88, 104, 105, 114
theirs 43
them 7, 14, 17, 18, 21–23, 31, 32, 34, 35, 37, 42, 43, 45–48, 51, 53, 54, 61, 62, 65, 67, 68, 82, 83, 94, 97, 100–103, 105
then 3, 6, 15, 16, 23, 31, 36, 44, 45, 49–51, 61, 64–66, 78, 79, 81, 84, 96, 103, 111
then-named 51
Theodore 79
theologically 56
theory 85, 93
therefore 19, 26, 35, 36, 46, 48, 49, 54, 63, 64, 100, 112
they 2–4, 6–9, 15, 16, 18–26, 28, 32, 35–38, 40, 41, 43, 45–48, 51–58, 60–64, 67, 68, 79, 81, 83–85, 87, 92, 94–96, 98, 100, 102, 111, 115
think 3, 5, 40, 43, 46, 97
Thorpe 92, 94, 98, 99, 101
those 2, 4–7, 9–12, 14, 15, 17, 23, 26, 31, 33, 34, 37, 39, 40, 42, 45, 47, 50, 52, 54, 56, 61, 62, 64–66, 68, 77, 79–83, 86, 87, 97–101, 104–106, 110, 112–116
thoughtful 115
thousand 100
threaten 52, 79
through 10, 11, 15, 21, 37, 45, 56, 60, 62, 67, 86, 92, 97, 103, 104, 116
thugs 83
ties 20
Tikkun 26, 28, 85, 86

For Product Safety Concerns and Information please contact our EU representative GPSR@taylorandfrancis.com
Taylor & Francis Verlag GmbH, Kaufingerstraße 24, 80331 München, Germany

www.ingramcontent.com/pod-product-compliance
Lightning Source LLC
Chambersburg PA
CBHW071822230426
43670CB00013B/2541

time 3, 11, 34, 35, 45, 48, 49, 51, 53, 55, 56, 66, 82, 83, 98, 101–104, 110, 114
Times of Israel 88
title 50, 64
today 1, 9, 17, 26, 35, 41, 44, 49, 56, 58, 67, 79, 86, 87, 96, 104
top-down 31
topics 1
toward 2, 6, 8, 10, 12, 21, 33, 36, 38, 40–42, 44, 51, 52, 55, 56, 66, 67, 82, 99, 114–116
tradition 2, 11, 14, 18, 19, 21, 23, 25, 35, 43, 49, 52, 53, 63, 77, 78, 81, 84, 96, 104, 112, 113
tragedies 51
tragedy 51
transcendent 16
transcript 116
translated 61
treated 34, 41, 86, 100
trends 10, 35, 54
tribes 18
true 17, 32, 48, 63, 112
truly 66
Trump 12, 33, 56, 61, 87, 88, 96
truthfully 105
trying 46, 83, 92, 93

turned 42, 68, 86, 111
tweet 111
twofold 19, 31
types 7, 15, 35, 51

Uganda 82
Ukraine 9, 36, 37, 53, 95
ultra-Orthodox 78, 81, 83, 87
undocumented immigration 61, 65, 88, 111
United Kingdom 39–41, 45, 85, 115
United Nations 1, 51
United States 1, 9–12, 15, 26, 27, 54–56, 77, 78, 84–87, 113

Vance, J.D. 33, 111, 112, 116
Vatican, The 10, 49, 50, 52, 68, 98
violence 7, 8, 12, 20, 23, 45, 52, 62, 63, 68, 79, 82, 86, 110, 115

Wolfe, Stephen 59
worship 55

xenophobia 8, 52, 87
xenos 66

Zionism 79, 81, 83